DAVE BRICKER

DEATH *of* THE GUITAR

COLLECTED STORIES, POEMS, & SKETCHES

Essential Absurdities Press

D A V E   B R I C K E R

DEATH *of* THE GUITAR

COLLECTED STORIES, POEMS, & SKETCHES

Copyright ©2019, Coral Gables, FL, USA

This book may not be reproduced, transmitted, or stored in whole or in part by any means, including graphic, electronic, or mechanical without the express written consent of the publisher except in the case of brief quotations embodied in critical articles and reviews.

Cover and book design by Dave Bricker.

ISBN: 978-0-9862960-3-1

ESSENTIAL ABSURDITIES PRESS

http://www.storysailing.com

for Eva

Table of Contents

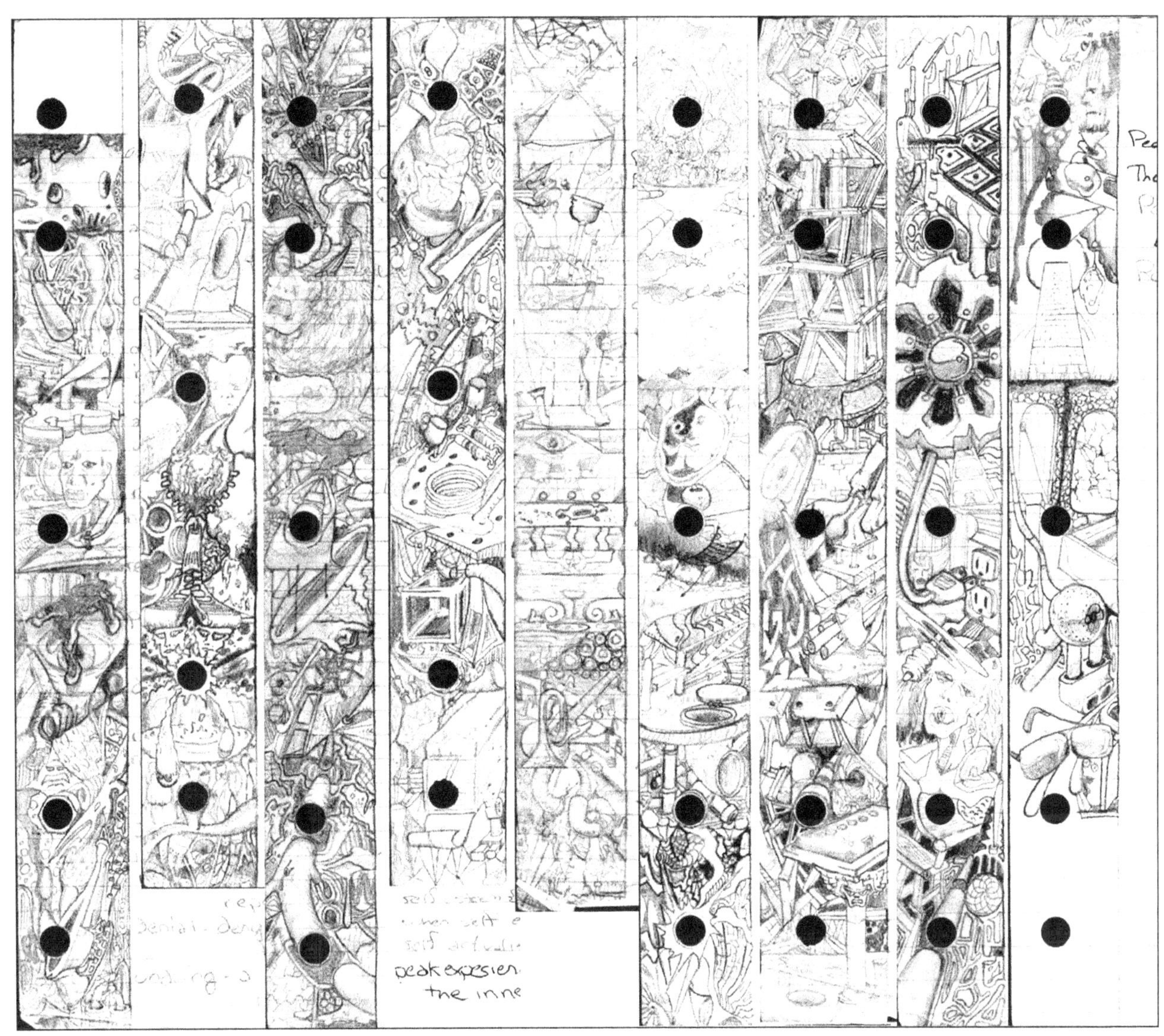

Continuous strip of margin sketches from high school psychology class, circa 1980

Introduction

PUBLISHING IS AN ENDEAVOR undertaken exclusively by people who have *something to say,* an unfortunate rarity in a world of so much content and so little substance. Whether your contribution to the world's literature is an aleatoric poem, a novel, a screenplay or a better software tutorial, it can change hearts, minds, lives, and fortunes, and inspire people to action, laughter, or tears.

As with any art, writing has inherent magical qualities, and technological resources now available to self-publishers enable the common magician to make his art available to ordinary people celebrating their right to literacy in a realm once the exclusive province of politicians and priests. Like any form of wisdom or spirit, the written word is not likely to be consumed until its potential beneficiary recognizes a thirst and makes his way to the water, but never in history has the stream of global consciousness and information been so accessible to contributions.

Much work is required: Documents must be formatted, covers designed, type set, and strategies planned – all of which actions are auxiliary to the creative, expository process we writers love. And yet, when you hold your own published book in your hands, leaf through its pages, and breathe the smell of fresh ink, you will know the satisfaction of having contributed to a process that connects the best of modern civilization to ancient Sumerians inscribing the first characters on a clay tablet with a reed stylus.

Writing is civilization, and printing is the dissemination of culture. The spread and growth of culture – wisdom, knowledge, and enlightenment in its many forms – is the winged horse bearing solutions to man's problems in troubled times. With millions of books already in print, the sole thing that might motivate us to contribute yet another is a conviction that we have a different insight, a new story, a divergent angle, a desire to contribute something *better.* And only through reading and writing will we ultimately come to understand ourselves, nurture the beautiful planet we are custodians of, and remember how to laugh in the darkness.

– *The One-Hour Guide to Self-Publishing* (2010)

Summer

August in Miami — a final, desperate campaign before October calls in the year's first cold front to break the back of summer's brutal occupation. The afternoon air is hot, muggy, penetrating, still. Heat waves dance wildly over black asphalt and gridlocked traffic. West of Miami, a vast wilderness of black water, cypress, and sawgrass stews in the summer heat. The water's surface is nearly 100°F. Evaporating moisture rises invisibly at first, cooling slowly as it gains altitude. Every thousand feet, the temperature falls 3.5°. Water vapor condenses into tiny droplets. A cloud forms, climbing higher, spreading outward and upward.

The cloud soon holds more cool, condensed water than it can carry. Rain streams beneath the cumulonimbus — a classic mushroom cloud — looming like Hiroshima's ghost over the land. Driven by high altitude winds, the thunderhead marches slowly toward open water. At fifty thousand feet, a stream of ice crystals blows off the top of the cloud bloom. Falling water collides with the still-rising heat, ascending into the sky again before ever hitting the ground.

Hot!

On Biscayne Bay in the anchorage, the air is heavy, thick, stifling. With no wind to blow them back on their mooring lines, the boats float at odd angles to one another. A tiny wake from a dinghy rowing in the channel spreads slowly, a thin black snake sidewinding across a flat desert of bright, reflected sky. Amplified by the silence, sonic wakes carried by thick, still air are as perceptible as their liquid counterparts. A clunking of oars in oar locks, a distant conversation, a cough – sounds normally too faint to be heard – skim across the hot glass bay.

Slack low tide. Inside the spoil islands in the dredged marina, the bottom is dark, grassless, and murky. Languid water bakes in the sun. Sheets of algae rise from the mud beneath the boats like fragments of old, rotten blanket. Lines hang loose. Boats sit motionless in their slips. Dock residents walk quickly along the white concrete edges of the piers, avoiding the wooden planks in the center. Heat rises from the boards as from a bed of coals. The scent of baking lumber hovers in the salt air.

The storm advances. Distant thunder rumbles from somewhere inland. In the shadow of the storm, the rising heat can no longer drive the rain back up into the sky. A gray curtain descends to earth.

Jerry St. Jacques and Ray Montana stand on their foredecks talking about the weather, their boats hanging in no particular direction. "Looks like we're gonna get another one," says Ray.

"Yep," says Jerry, "and I hope that sonofabitch over there with his piece-of-crap boats and twisted-up anchor lines doesn't drift down on anyone when the wind comes up."

Jerry's referring to the collection of quasi-abandoned boats in the middle of the anchorage – salvaged, stolen, or otherwise unofficially owned by Crazy Jim – tied together and covered with broken dinghies, old masts and rigging, faded fenders, broken outboards, and a thick layer of cormorant scat. Nobody's quite sure how his horrible collection of jetsam is fastened to the bottom, but a coil of frayed and twisted lines as thick as a man's leg extends from the bow of the central hulk down into the water.

"I swear I'm gonna cut all that junk loose some dark night when there's a west wind blowing," says Ray.

Jerry laughs. It's something we all threaten to do under our breath, especially when the most innocent exchange with Crazy Jim provokes a screaming, cursing rage about his "rights." But though we'd love to see him and his trash collection go, as sailors, we don't have it in us to cut anyone's lines, however poorly tended they might be.

The thunderhead obscures the sun.

The air turns green. The light is vivid, unusual, clear, as if frequencies not normally visible can be perceived. An electric presence charges the atmosphere, an excitement. We're at the edge of something not quite identifiable that inspires vigilance, alertness, a note of fear. Summer squalls don't last long but they can blow with hurricane force.

A bright crackle-flash of lightning accompanies an enormous boom of thunder.

That one must have hit the marina.

A single halyard clangs nervously against a mast somewhere.

A second one joins in.

The tinkling sound spreads slowly, subtly, across the piers and out through the anchorage – a mad chorus of warning bells.

The temperature plummets.

A low humming of vibrating lines and rigging rises beneath the chorus of ringing halyards.

A cold blast of air jerks our boats back on their anchors. A few, caught broadside by the gust, heel awkwardly and sail forward until, arrested by their mooring lines, they fall back with the others.

I insert all but the top drop-board into my companionway, then pull the main hatch closed over my head as the first fat raindrops spatter against my wooden cockpit locker top.

Another blast of wind rips through the anchorage. My neighbor's wind generator spins up with a hissy growl.

More rain.

Lines and rigging hum, vibrating like the strings of an instrument resonating through the air-filled hulls to which they are affixed. When the wind reaches a certain speed, when the vibrations are just so, the rigging harmonizes awkwardly, producing what violin makers call a 'wolf tone.' *Blue Monk* pumps as if played by a gigantic bow.

Lightning strikes again somewhere close, close enough to hear it sizzle as it flashes and explodes. I comfort myself thinking about how many other boats in the anchorage have taller masts than mine.

The edge of the cloud is above us now.

Dark.

Cold air falls and collides with the earth, spreading across the water as jets of wet wind. I watch through the top companionway board slot. The curtain of rain advances from shore, obscuring the buildings in Coconut Grove, then the tops of the masts of boats in the marina behind the spoil islands. The island behind me disappears.

I'm in it now.

Charged by fast-moving air, the bay whips into an angry chop. Anchored boats hobbyhorse wildly, straining at their lines. Salt spray and rain obscure my view through the ports on the cabin sides; I have no forward-facing windows. If a boat blows down on me, I won't see it coming. I'm dry, but in my foul weather jacket and pants, I sweat in my stuffy cabin, straining to see the boats around me, looking for changes in their relative positions and angles to the wind that might indicate dragging anchors – theirs or mine.

A blast sounds from a horn somewhere. There's nothing I can do to help; I have only my rowing dinghy. I hope nobody drags down on me but I won't venture out unless I must.

After a few minutes, the wind blows itself out. Water spirals down the cockpit drains. The rain falls steadily but gently now, calming the sea. The torrent fades to a drizzle, then a sprinkle, and finally moves on across the bay.

The air remains humid but the temperature is cooler now. I open my hatch, remove the drop-boards and climb out to the cockpit, stripping off my rain gear. A small sailboat has blown up on the island. A shirtless man stands next to it in ankle-deep water, his hands on his hips. He's lucky; it's low tide and his boat has a shallow draft. He'll set some anchors and tow her off at high tide no worse for the wear.

Crazy Jim's collection of junk still floats here in all its glory.

A breath of light, easterly breeze fills in. Anchorites open hatches and raise wind scoops. The easy chop we're accustomed to returns. With it comes the gentle, soothing, hypnotic slapping of waves against our bows.

Jerry comes out on deck and hollers over to Ray Montana, "I clocked sixty-three knots on my wind indicator."

"I'm not surprised," Ray returns, "but at least it cooled things down."

"Amen," says Jerry. "Amen to that."

"Hey Dave," Ray calls over to me, "I've got a cooler full of ice here. Come on over."

I smile back, shoot him a thumbs-up, bail out my half-sunk dinghy, and row over to join him.

Ray gestures toward the tall buildings in Coconut Grove. "I wonder what it's like to be in a storm high up in one of those big condo towers over there?" He descends into his cabin and then follows two cold glasses up through the companionway to join me in the cockpit.

"They probably don't even notice," I conjecture.

"That's too bad," he says. "That's too bad."

– *The Blue Monk,* 2016

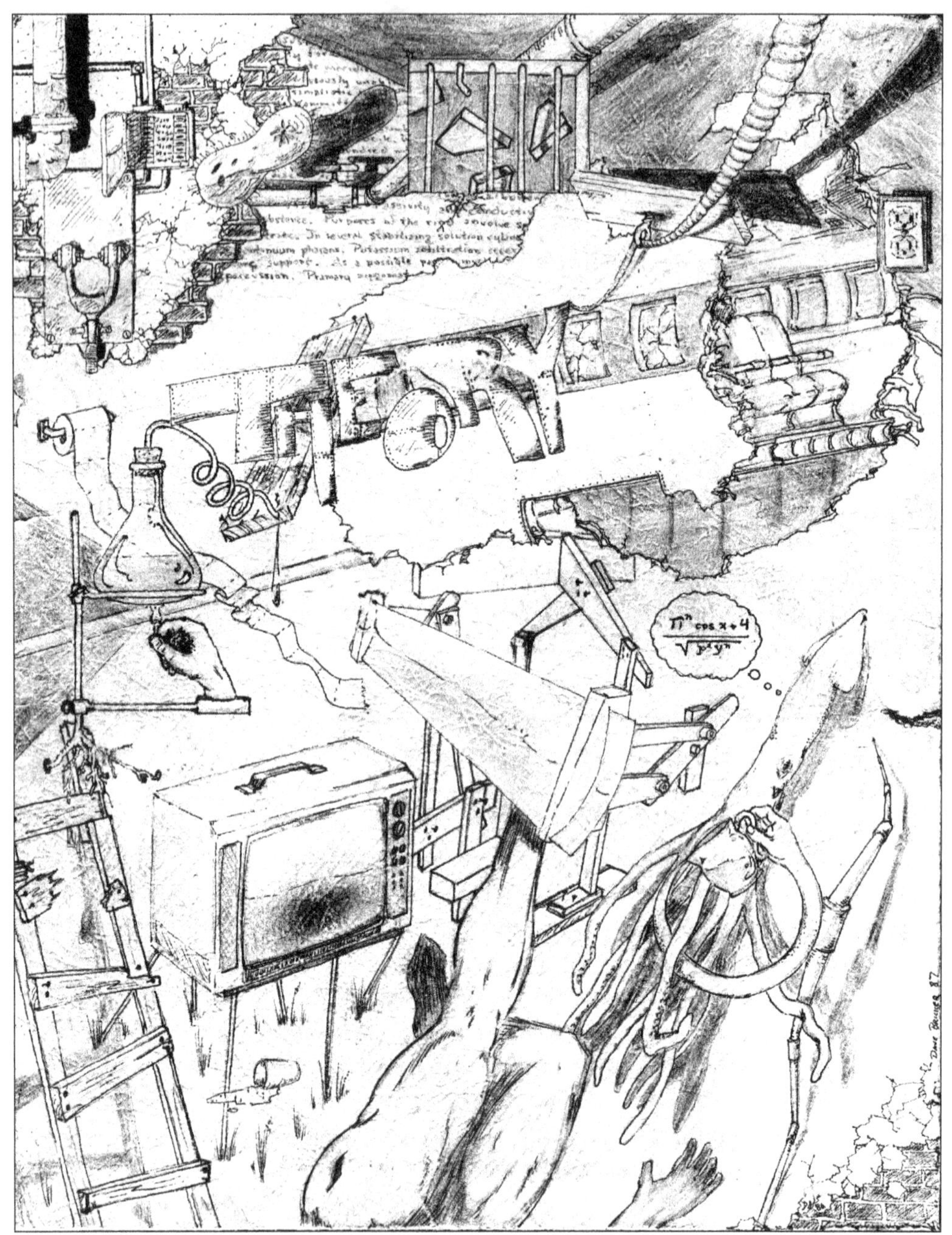

College Music Theory class notebook cover, 1987

Stone Soup

2017

In November, 1954
In Sylacauga, Alabama
Ann Hodges was lying on her couch
Asleep
In her apartment
In the middle of the afternoon
With a blanket wrapped around her
And a cylindrical couch cushion wedged under her neck
When a meteorite
Or a baseball-sized piece of one
(Isn't a *piece* of a meteorite still a "meteorite?")
Crashed through the ceiling
Bounced off the radio
And made a bruise the size and shape of a pineapple on her side

Death of the Guitar

The reporters said the space rock
Was twelve inches in *circumference*
Reporters like to exaggerate
Twelve inches sounds big
But if we divide 12 by pi (3.14 is good enough)
We can calculate that the *diameter* of the Hodges meteorite
Was 3.8 inches
More like a softball than a baseball
But a lot less like an iron basketball than you might think
If you're not paying attention

Ann Hodges' landlord was named Birdie Guy
(I think that's a great name; don't you?
Especially for a woman)
"Birdie, this is Ann. How are you?"
"Good to hear from you, Ann
Is everything okay?"
"Yeah, I'm fine
But there's this big hole in the ceiling
And you're not going to believe how it got there!"

Everyone came over to Ann Hodges' apartment
Neighbors
Reporters
Her sister

The Brattles came over
From the white house three doors down
The one with the pillars in front
And the circular driveway
And the mailbox with a big decal of a largemouth bass on it
"It's a good thing it didn't hit *our* house," said Ernie Brattle
"It could have hit one of the children
Or dented the hood of my new Packard"
"This is God's judgment," proclaimed Millicent Brattle
"It didn't hit *our* house because nobody was home
Nobody was idly sleepin' in our house
When they coulda been bein' *productive*"

Billy Hodges from around the block
(Same last name but no relation)

And his friend Dewey
Saw the cars in front of the apartment
They threw their bikes down on the front lawn
And hung around for a few minutes
And thought it was kind of cool
That a rock from space
Could punch a hole in the ceiling
"I wonder what the odds of being hit by a meteorite are?" mused Dewey
Billy suggested they were "astronomical"
And they laughed
And got a few dirty looks
Because this was a *serious matter*
They left after a few minutes
When the thrill wore off

A geologist analyzed the rock
And found high concentrations of iron and nickel
He confirmed that the rock was indeed a meteorite
A visitor from outer space
Woooooooo

People in town had seen smoke trails in the sky
And some heard a *boom*
When the meteor broke the sound barrier
A few thought a plane had crashed
Walter Emmons conjectured
That the soviets were responsible
And told everyone to get ready
For President Eisenhower to make a move against the commies

Sergeant Drake of the Sylacauga Police Force
Said the rock was "evidence"
He confiscated it
And called in the experts from the U.S. Air Force
Who know all about rocks from space
(Because they fly jets at very high altitudes, I guess)
And they also confirmed
That the Hodges meteorite was
In fact
A meteorite

Death of the Guitar

Walter Emmons was disappointed
He'd spent a lot of money on ammunition
And had stocked up his cellar
With emergency food supplies

When Ann got out of the hospital…

Well, she didn't go there because of the injury
She went there because all the lookie-loos
And rubberneckers
And gawkers and neighbors
And reporters asking questions
Made her anxious
And nervous
And *frenzied*
And she needed a sedative

But anyway …
When Ann got out of the hospital
And all the commotion had died down

She wanted her meteorite back
Her meteorite
But her landlady
Birdie Guy
(The one with the interesting name)
Wanted to keep it for herself
After all, it had fallen on *her* property
And I'm sure it wasn't cheap to fix the roof
Birdie hired a lawyer
And sued Ann Hodges

But folks thought it was unfair
When you're struck by a rock from space
You've been *chosen*
You – not your landlady
You should get to keep it
After all
If Ann Hodges had been hit by a stray bullet
While napping on her couch
It's not like Birdie Guy would have come around

And claimed the bullet belonged to her
Even if she did have to pay
To fix the hole in the wall

They settled out of court for 500 bucks
500 bucks
That's $4,364.53 in today's money
For a softball-sized chunk of iron from outer space
That might have landed in the Indian Ocean
Or on a glacier in Alaska
Or on some mountainside in Tibet
Or perhaps in Bulgaria

But by that time
The Christmas holidays had come and gone
And Rosa Parks had been arrested in Montgomery
And Salk's new polio vaccine was in the news
And Disneyland was about to open
And Ernie Brattle had put a big crease
In the right rear quarter panel of his new Packard

And the Bureau of Engraving had added “In God We Trust”
To all of our nation’s paper currency

Nobody made an offer
To buy Ann’s softball-sized chunk of rock from space
So she donated it to a museum
And went back to sleep
All cozy and safe
In her apartment
With a blanket wrapped around her
And a cylindrical couch cushion wedged under her neck

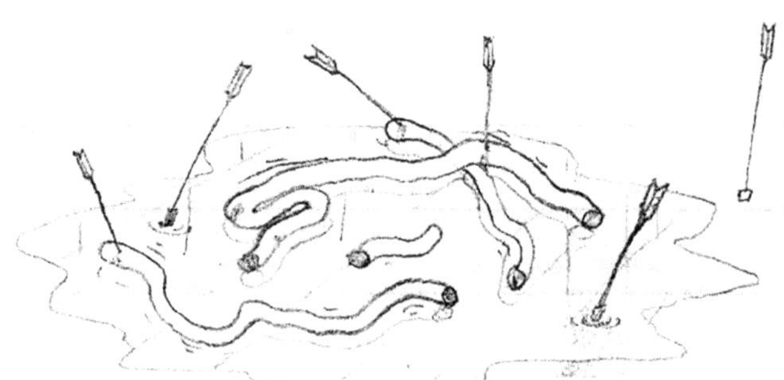

High school sketch, circa 1980

Death of the Guitar

TINO LANDED ON THE INSTRUMENT with heels together. The top buckled and collapsed. Fractured pieces of cypress and cedar tumbled weightless in space. The neck and fingerboard rotated and separated, suddenly released from the tension of the strings. The bridge bounced off Tino's boot. An ebony tuning peg towed a thin white spiral of guitar string skyward before hitting the end of its tether and tumbling crazily back. A thin veil of dust and time-suspended wood particles hovered over the imploding instrument.

The scream of the dying guitar was dramatic – sudden – like the death of a living thing – the liberation of a soul. A visceral crunch and the sound of a single note broke the room – or perhaps the sound of all possible notes at once. No fundamental, nameable pitch was distinguishable, only a percussive ring followed by a clash of overtones. Harmonics bounced off walls like a blind genie frantically escaping a hot brass lamp, echoing interminably, and finally yielding to a hollow, profound, and equally overpowering silence.

Nobody said a word … except Tino who raised a hand to his forehead. "*Muerto,*" he said. "Dead. I could not allow either of us to suffer."

Time, capsized, righted itself. The hum of the lights became audible. Everyone drew a deep breath. The room came back into focus.

In the shadows, on the floor next to the shattered guitar, with eyes wide like saucers sat young Andreas, Hanns's brass hammer still gripped tight in his trembling hand.

– *The Dance*, 2009

Everything You Know is a Story

"INTERESTING, and I'm glad you mentioned time, Vincent. Who here thinks the future exists?"

"It probably doesn't," said Kaitlin. "It hasn't happened yet."

"Does the past exist?"

"I think only in our memories – in recorded form," offered Doug.

"So the only thing that truly exists is the moment – the tiny instant of now?"

"It's hard to imagine it," said Audrey, "but logic suggests it's true; truth is an instant – a point. The past is gone and the future hasn't happened yet."

"So if messages take time to get to you, everything you think you know technically no longer exists. You can only perceive past events – and they're gone.

"Back to Lenore, our physicist: What happens if you slow matter down to absolute zero degrees Kelvin – if you slow it down to where all molecular motion stops – which is essentially what happens when the Universe exists in a single moment?"

"It falls apart. It collapses into fundamental particles of matter and en…"

"So as promised, I have just destroyed the Universe."

"Where's the kaboom?" asked Doug in a cartoon voice. "There was supposed to be an earth-shattering kaboom!"

The happiness delegates laughed, grateful for a moment of relief from Strider's philosophical gyrations.

"But since we haven't all collapsed into a haze of quarks and neutrinos and electrons and protons and morons and such, perhaps one of our assumptions is wrong? Maybe the past and the future do exist?

"What do you mean?" asked Micky Tomm.

"Maybe we can think of time as a river – as a continuum. If we put a clock on a spaceship that travels very fast, when the traveling clock returns, it will show an earlier time than clocks that remained on Earth – it ticks more slowly relative to the stationary clock – and I say 'relative," because the so-called 'stationary' clock on earth is still rotating around the earth's axis and whizzing around the sun like we are. The same is true about the wristwatches of a standing person and a walking person, but the time difference is too tiny to measure."

"Einstein called this 'relativistic time,'" explained Lenore. "Events that occur at one time for one observer can occur at different times for another. He talked about space and time as being interwoven. According to Einstein's special relativity, any object that has mass causes a distortion in space-time – which is responsible for what we call 'gravity.' One quasar about 8 billion light-years from Earth sits behind a galaxy that is 400 million light-years away. Four different images of that same quasar appear around the galaxy because the intense gravity of the galaxy bends the light that comes from it. Astronomers call it 'Einstein's Cross.'"

Walter broke in. "This science lesson under the stars is interesting, but what does it have to do with happiness, connection, engagement, or your Essential Absurdities, Strider?"

"My point is that everything you know is a story," Strider raised his index finger. "And it's a story built from flimsy evidence; our senses are inadequate. The human eye can only see about 38,000 colors; the average computer monitor can display over sixteen-million. Only a tiny range of the spectrum of energy is visible to our eyes. Imagine what the world would look like if we could see X-rays and ultraviolet and infrared. Is that picture of the world truer than the one we perceive? Our senses only receive past tense information; we can't perceive what's happening now. Our clocks all tick at different speeds.

"These are the Essential Absurdities – things we can never see directly – things we draw conclusions about based on their effects on what we can see – magic forces we struggle to understand and explain with tools and instruments and brains that aren't up to the task.

"Take connection for example. How do you explain what that is? What does it mean to look into a lover's eyes? What does it mean when we call someone a friend? What does it mean when four hundred people sitting in church feel like they're part of a community? What does it mean when a woman in California calls her identical twin sister in Germany because she 'feels something is wrong' and finds out she's sick? Does connection even mean the same thing to you as it does to me?

"And then what is meaning? What does it mean to ask, 'What does it mean?'?

"The world is full of mysteries – things science or the senses will never adequately explain. We give them labels like 'God,' 'love', 'self,' 'connection,' – 'truth' – and we throw these labels around as if they mean anything we can remotely comprehend. All these things are stories – and if you happen to love those stories, I'm not saying they're not valid; I'm just saying that stories are the building blocks we use to construct our world. Stories bring us closer to the Mystery. Stories help us deal with the enormity of the Universe. Everything you know or think you know is a story."

– The Story Story, 2018

Words of Encouragement

February, 2016

My young pen pal (I help her with her English homework.) in the Middle East was feeling a bit down on herself. We've all seen the lists of fluffy aphorisms and pat-on-the-back sayings that circulate endlessly in tiring email chain letters. You'll have to judge for yourself whether or not there's any substance in my own list of observations about the world, but here are my original words of encouragement. I hope they give you a smile.

- Don't try to be like anyone except the best *you* you can be. You're the world's leading expert on that. As special as you are, you'd make a terrible me, and I'd do a horrible job being you.

- We all question ourselves, and there's usually no shortage of people who doubt you and remind you of your shortcomings. These people project their own self-doubts onto you. If you believe them, you fall into the trap of pitying yourself. There's no need. Unlearn the belief that you are imperfect; that kind of thinking has no place in your life. Your flaws and weaknesses are part of your perfection.

- Today is the first day of the rest of your life. What will you make of it? How will you inspire someone? What can you do that will be kind and helpful? How can you make your life – and the lives of others – richer by living well?

- Make some effort each day to acknowledge your own good qualities – even if you don't believe in them 100%. Cook yourself a nice dinner. Or skip dessert. Take a yoga class or go jogging or walking or ride your bike. Extend at least one positive gesture to yourself every day; make that a habit. Positive people attract positive people. Be one. Now.

- People who try to please everybody make the world bland, boring, and unflavored while they fail to accomplish their impossible objective. Satisfied people usually smile and quietly move on. The only way you can know for sure that you're making an impact is when someone gets upset. Rile people up a little bit. They need it.

- Be honest with people who can handle truth. Be silent and understanding with the rest.

- Dream. Head in the right direction and put one foot in front of the other. The top of the mountain will have no choice but to come to you.

- You don't need money to accomplish meaningful goals. Don't invent obstacles. I have climbed mountains, slept inside a volcano, swum with whales, sailed across an ocean in a wooden boat, written books, and passed my sense of mischief and love of the Mystery on to my daughter who will be sneaking thumbtacks onto God's chair long after I'm gone. Adventure lies in every direction. All you have to do is step off the sidewalk into the woods.

- Make a story out of your life. Fill it with engaging characters, great adventures, beautiful scenery, daunting challenges, love, heartbreak, and triumph. Be an amazing protagonist. Live each day as if you're going to publish and share it … then publish and share it.

- Your friends will be there for you; you won't have to ask them. Be there for them and your true friends will reveal themselves in time.

- Write down your fears and discard the ones that start with, "What if ...?" Most are products of your imagination. Take the rest out into the world with you. If you're not scared, you're not living. The only fear that empowers is fear of regret. Being brave and courageous has nothing to do with not being scared.

- God has a sense of humor and a thick skin. Anyone who jumps to his defense or appoints themselves his personal advertising agency has neither faith nor spiritual confidence. Does the elephant need the devoted ant's protection?

- Only a fearful and twisted person could write the myth of hell. If you die and it goes like the book says and God really turns out to be such a horrible and cruel and sociopathic barbarian that he would submit people to *eternal* pain, fire, and torment, tell him I deceived you; it's all my fault and I should go in your place.

- The beauty of God, art, and love is that they can't be defined. Spend your life pondering, wondering, exploring, and experiencing but avoid the false comfort of forming hard conclusions about how the Universe works. Joy, magic, and wonder are found in the Mystery – not in pretending to know the unknowable.

- Don't believe what you've been told about "those people." They're just like you.

- Remember that for all the world's problems, this is the best time in human history to have ever lived – and that you were lucky enough to thread the needle of time. Not long ago, there was no air travel or antibiotics. Anesthesia and the Internet are historically recent inventions. You can drive your own air-conditioned car on a paved road from Miami to Alaska. We listen to musicians who died decades before we were born. I have electricity and clean running water in my home. How much of that existed a hundred years ago? And flush toilets rock.

- Don't spend too much time seeking enlightenment. It will return to you when you stop yearning for it and learn to just be.

- Solving all the world's problems starts with being a tiny, happy, healthy part of it. Don't worry about the rest until you've accomplished step 1.

- The world is full of poetry you won't understand at first. Listen to Charlie Parker or Thelonious Monk or stare at a Picasso until you *get it.* (Chopin or Zappa will work, too)

- If you don't play an instrument, sing, clap your hands, or whistle. If you do play an instrument, learn to play it in tune and in time so you can touch and share the Mystery. A single note, played with passion, can convey the entire Universe.

- Surround yourself with positive, powerful, constructive people who succeed and want you to succeed. Keep the rest at arm's length without losing your compassion for them.

- Find out where your food and other stuff comes from. Follow it from farm, forest, or fishery to the factory to the store to your table. Make informed decisions that have ethical and positive consequences for you, the environment, future generations, and the good people who struggle to offer you alternatives and solutions. Insert yourself into the chain and become a healthy link.

- Try not to answer a question as it was stated. The best answers are usually reframed questions.

- Your new Porsche will be shredded for scrap metal one day. *You* can opt for cremation.

- You *can* usually judge a book by its cover.
- If you really want to learn something, teach it.
- Beware of people who enthusiastically seek leadership positions. Anyone qualified doesn't want the job.
- Remind yourself occasionally that the world isn't made of pixels.
- It's better to ride around on a garbage truck with kind people every day than it is to work with idiots.
- You don't have to fight for every worthy cause. Sometimes it's easier to wait for a bad idea to collapse under the weight of its own stupidity.
- Always ask, "Why not?"
- Be skeptical of advice that begins with "Always" or "Never."
- Read a lot, but don't waste too much time reading long lists of other people's philosophies, especially if the weather's nice.

- Sooner or later, you'll step in shit. Clean off your shoe and move on.
- Embrace aging; it beats the alternative.
- Life is absurd. If you're not laughing, you're not learning.
- Learn interesting or silly new vocabulary words - just for fun. A "hippopotomonstrosesquipedaliophile" is a lover of very long words. The flap of skin at the tip of your elbow is called a "weenus."
- Pay attention to kerning.
- Imagine how free you would be if you owned nothing.
- Fall in love (it usually takes a few tries).
- Say something ridiculous once in a while just to shake things up.
- Plastic acorn anonymous wizard apron.

- Spend a night sleeping under the stars.
- Avoid fast food.
- Floss every day.

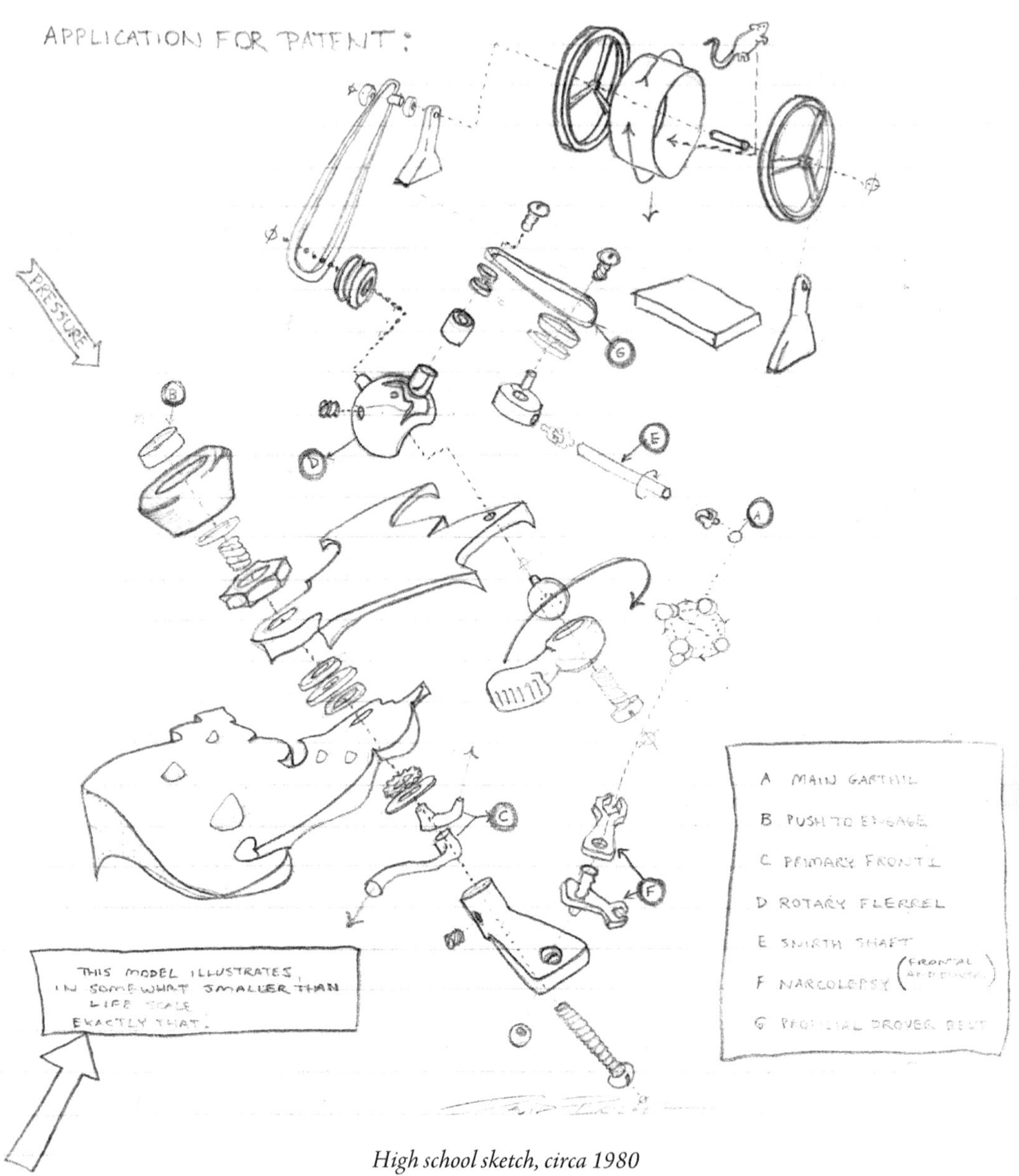

High school sketch, circa 1980

The Truth About Christmas

A Holiday Parable, 2016

JEFFERSON BAUGH DESPISED CHRISTMAS. He hated the incessant month-long cacophony of pop-music-infused holiday carols that began the day after Thanksgiving and droned on through New Years. He loathed holiday sales and the annual cycle of rampant commercialism. He scoffed at animated Christmas shows featuring doe-eyed children who found their way home *because they believed.* And at fifteen years of age, gifts "from Santa" disgusted him. Christmas was phony, hypocritical, insincere, and absurd.

Jefferson ignored the half-dozen student presentations that preceded his own, thinking of them as so many stepping-stones on the path toward winter break – a respite from teachers, classrooms, homework, and morons wearing elf hats and reindeer antler hairbands that could not come too soon. A final *"Feliz Navidad"* slide ended Maria Perez's agonizing presentation on Puerto Rican Holiday Traditions. The sprinkle of polite classroom applause faded.

Miss Hamilton took a deep breath followed by an unintentionally audible sigh. "Mr. Baugh, what do you have to show us today?"

Jefferson approached the front of the class – not so slowly that he could be accused of stalling, but just slowly enough to inspire a note of tension in the room. His disheveled hair, carelessly tucked-in shirt, and the hole in the thigh of his well-worn jeans suggested that despite his many hours of research, Jefferson was not prepared to deliver his presentation.

But he *was* prepared – prepared to meet Christmas head-on. Miss Hamilton's "holiday presentation" assignment offered the perfect opportunity to state his case against hollow traditions and "un-Christian practices" – not that he was at all religious – but Jefferson had armed himself with facts – inarguable, incontestable, undeniable facts. What self-respecting person would dare contradict conclusions derived from *truth?* Jefferson was confident of victory over the dark forces of ignorance.

He fumbled in his pocket for his thumb drive and plugged it awkwardly into the computer at the front of the classroom, double-clicked, and waited for his presentation to launch. His title slide, "The Truth About Christmas" shone in stark, white, sans-serif type against an uninspiring gray-to-black gradient background.

"What the hell does a dimwit like you know about Christmas?" heckled Greg Highland from the second-to-last row.

"Maybe Santa will bring you a brain this year," added Bill Hagstrom.

Jefferson smiled. "Don't worry. I used short words and big text. I'll try to speak slowly so…"

"That's enough" interrupted Miss Hamilton, peering over her glasses. Mr. Baugh, please proceed."

Jefferson inhaled and began. "The Truth About Christmas," he recited, ignoring the fact that everyone already knew full well what his presentation was about. He waited another awkward moment before continuing.

"Today, I'd like to reveal the true origins of three popular Christmas stories and traditions – Christmas trees, mistletoe, and the origin of Santa Claus."

"How can the origin of Santa Claus be the origin of something else," interrupted Jeanne Sharpington, but Miss Hamilton arrested her with a stare and nodded to Jefferson to disengage and proceed.

An image of a logging camp faded onto the screen.

"Christmas Trees," he stated, repeating the caption.

"According to the National Christmas Tree Association, 25–30 million *real* Christmas trees are sold in the United States every year. It can take as many as fifteen years to grow a tree of typical height (6–7 feet), but the average growing time is seven years.[1]

He clicked to a slide with a big green question mark on it that followed the word "Responsible." "Is it environmentally responsible to cut down *30 million* trees every year?

Leaving that question unanswered, Jefferson clicked again to reveal another question rendered in white text against the dark background. "But most important...," he prompted the class, "What do Christmas Trees have to do with Christmas?

A photo of "The Holy Bible" appeared.

Jefferson cleared his throat. "The Prophet Jeremiah *condemned* the ancient Middle Eastern practice of cutting down trees, bringing them home, and decorating them as *pagan.*

"Of course, those weren't really Christmas trees, because Jesus wasn't born until centuries later, but in Jeremiah's time, the 'heathen' would cut down trees, carve or decorate them in the form of gods or goddesses, and overlay them with precious metals.

A scanned image of an open Bible followed. Jefferson quoted scripture, stretching his arms out and forward as if to deliver his congregation from unholy sin.

"Jeremiah 10:2-4: Thus sayeth the Lord, Learn not the way of the heathen, and be not dismayed at the signs of heaven; for the heathen are dismayed at them. For the customs of the people are vain: for one cutteth a tree out of the forest, the work of the hands of the workman, with the axe. They deck it with silver and with gold; they fasten it with nails and with hammers, that it move not."

Bob Parks in the second row stood up. "You're gonna burn in hell, you ..."

"Mr. Parks," interjected Miss Hamilton. "If you...."

"What's your problem, Parks?" Jefferson protested. "It's not like I changed what it says in the Bible. If you don't like that Christmas trees are for heathens, go see your shrink ... or your parole officer ... or go hassle a priest about it."

"Stop!" shouted the teacher. "Jefferson, please go on."

"It wasn't until 1851 that Pastor Henry Schwan of Cleveland, Ohio decorated the first Christmas tree in an American church. His parishioners condemned it as a pagan practice. Some even threatened him with violence."

The next slide displayed a clip-art glowing light bulb with the word "Conclusions" beneath it. Jefferson revealed his bullet points one at a time.

- Christmas trees disregard life and waste precious resources.

- Christmas trees started as a form of pagan worship.
- Christmas trees are condemned by the Bible as "heathen."
- The tradition of decorating Christmas trees in the US is historically recent.
- Despite their popularity, Christmas trees have *nothing* to do with Christmas.[2]

Miss Hamilton nestled her chin into her elbow-supported hands and closed her eyes.

A cheerful illustration of a smiling young man and woman about to kiss in a doorway beneath a sprig of mistletoe slid onto the screen. "Mistletoe," recited Jefferson. "What does mistletoe have to do with Christmas?"

"The story of mistletoe comes from Norse mythology."[3] A comic book Thor character dropped onto the screen.

"Mistletoe was the sacred plant of Frigga, goddess of love and mother of Baldur, god of the summer sun. Baldur had a dream of death that alarmed his mother, for should he die, all life would perish. Frigga went to the elements – air, fire, water, and earth – and to every animal and plant, asking them to promise that no harm would come to Baldur. All agreed.

"But Loki, god of evil, knew of one plant Frigga had overlooked. Loki made an arrow tip out of mistletoe and shot Baldur dead.

"The elements tried to bring Baldur back to life. Frigga finally revived him. Her tears turned into the white berries on the mistletoe plant, and in her joy, Frigga kissed everyone who passed beneath the tree on which the mistletoe grew. She decreed that no harm should befall anyone standing under the mistletoe. Instead, a kiss should be given as token of love."

Jefferson paused to take in the annoyed faces of his classmates, and relish his audience's captivity before proceeding.

Jefferson's "giant question mark" motif returned. "What does mistletoe have to do with Christmas?" he asked his classmates.

"Ain't nobody gonna kiss a dumb-ass like you without some sorta excuse," offered Bob Parks.

Jefferson rolled his eyes and smirked as Miss Hamilton motioned sideways toward the door with her thumb. Parks marched himself self-righteously out of the room.

- Mistletoe has its origins in Norse mythology.

- Mistletoe is a parasitic plant that's propagated through bird poop.

- Mistletoe has no connection whatsoever to biblical Christianity.

"Jefferson, exactly what is your point?" queried Miss Hamilton.

"I have one more topic. If you'll let me finish, I'll get to the conclusion when I..."

"Okay ... okay, continue," urged the teacher. Despite her wish to move on, Miss Hamilton recognized that Jefferson Baugh had – uncharacteristically – done his research, designed his slides (even if they weren't very good), and arrived on time to deliver his assignment.

A jolly, red-faced Saint Nick appeared on-screen. "Santa Claus," Jefferson began, "is perhaps the most interesting Christmas story of all."

"Poor Santa," sighed Haley Martin.

"Legend has it that Santa and his outfit were designed by Coca Cola. He made his first appearance in early-20th century ads, and this defined the way he looks today.

"But Santa's origins go back farther than that." Jefferson paused for dramatic effect.

"Santa's red robe and his bag of goodies, his sleigh, his flying reindeer, and his coming down the chimney all began with the ancestral traditions of the

Kamchadale and Koryak indigenous peoples of Siberia." Jefferson eviscerated the pronunciations of the names of the tribes, but Miss Hamilton thought better of mentioning it.

"At least there's *some* truth to this story," Jefferson intoned. "Santa really does come from the North Pole!" Jefferson looked at his classmates and smiled, mischievously hoping they'd find some solace in his last revelation before he dropped the boom.

"Have you seen the traditional red and white mushrooms in fairytale illustrations – toadstools? *Muscaria* mushrooms lie at the heart of the Santa story. These mushrooms are poisonous, but when dried out, they're not dangerous."

Jefferson clicked over to a Norman Rockwell painting of Christmas stockings hanging over a fireplace. "The tribal shaman" would dry the mushrooms out by hanging them in a sock over the fire. *That's* where the tradition of Christmas stockings began."

The next slide featured flying reindeer pulling Santa's sleigh across a full-moon sky.

"Reindeer *love* to eat *muscaria* mushrooms. The Arctic people observed that when reindeer consumed these mushrooms, they'd leap high into the air and prance around. This is why Santa's sleigh is pulled by flying reindeer in today's version of the story … and obviously, the mushrooms had some unusual effect on the reindeer's behavior."

"When people saw the fun the reindeer were having and tried eating the mushrooms themselves, they discovered the mushrooms had powerful hallucinogenic properties … but the mushrooms also caused stomach cramps – really *bad* stomach cramps. A picture of a toilet slid onto the screen.

"But some brave person observed that the reindeer didn't have that problem. And if you let the reindeer eat the mushrooms first, they'd absorb all the toxins and pee out all the hallucinogens. Shamans began to get high … by drinking reindeer urine."

"That's just *gross,*" remarked Haley Martin.

Miss Hamilton crossed her arms. "Really, Jefferson, is this necessary? I …"

"I'm sorry if the story is a little unsettling," replied Jefferson, "but it's not like I'm making this stuff up. I'm just reporting the truth. Isn't that what academic research is supposed to…?"

"And you're almost done?" cringed Miss Hamilton.

"Yes, Ma'am. Just … just a few more slides."

Miss Hamilton nodded.

Another image of Santa in a red and white robe graced the screen. "When the shaman would go out to collect mushrooms, he'd wear a red and white ceremonial robe in honor of the mushroom's colors.

The next slide showed Santa on a rooftop with a big bag of gifts. "He'd collect mushrooms in a large sack along with some reindeer pee, then return to his yurt – which was sort of like a round teepee or tent where the village elders gathered for the ceremony.

Jefferson clicked over to a photo of a modern-day yurt in Lapland. "What do you do when you live in the Arctic and your door is blocked by four or five feet of snow? You climb up on the roof to the hole where the smoke escapes, and you slide down the lodge pole to get in. That's where the whole crazy tradition of Santa dragging a bag of gifts down the chimney really came from."

"Question mark slide!" shouted Bob Durmond a moment before Jefferson clicked the remote and validated that prophesy. The class tittered, grateful for a note of comic relief.

"What does Santa Claus have to with Christmas?" continued Jefferson as he tried to conceal his irritation over having been second-guessed. He began to recite his bullet points.[4]

Santa Claus is a symbolic retelling of a psychedelic mushroom ritual that originated with Arctic tribal peoples.

Santa Claus has nothing to do with Christianity or Biblical tradition or Christmas.

Santa Claus…

"Thank you, Mr. Baugh," interrupted Miss Hamilton.

"But I…"

"Thank you, but we're out of time. We have a lot of presentations to get through and..."

"But..."

"Jefferson Baugh, please return to your seat. I will see you after class to discuss your presentation *and* your grade. That will be all."

Jefferson shuffled to his desk in the back row, stumbling over Bob Durmond's extended foot on the way.

Indignation over having been shot down for what he felt was a legitimate, truthful, and well-researched presentation banished all awareness of the ones that followed. *I'm sorry those idiots don't like the truth, but they shouldn't penalize me for pointing out the hypocrisy of their cherished little traditions.*

Miss Hamilton pilloried him after class and called his presentation "inappropriate" and "in poor taste." He listened with feigned politeness, offering "Yes, Ma'am"s and "No Ma'am"s in response to her tirade. Suspecting correctly that quoting Jesus's edict about "Seek the truth..." would not help his case, he endured her lecture and finally, with relief, walked out of the classroom into halls that had emptied of students for the day.

He donned his jacket, slung his book bag over his shoulder, and strode out onto the snowy sidewalk to begin the half-mile trek home.

Two blocks down, Bob Parks, Greg Highland, and Bill Hagstrom ambushed him with a barrage of slushy snowballs. Blinded, he could do nothing to stop them from hurling his book bag onto a nearby fire escape. Bob Parks knocked him down with a blow to his left eye and kicked him repeatedly. "That's from Santa," said Highland. "Merry Christmas. I hope you enjoy your reindeer piss," jeered Hagstrom.

Jefferson lay stunned on the pavement in the snow and ice as his assailants moved on and their voices faded. *I wonder if my ribs are broken.* He sat up slowly, cleared the snow from his face, and tentatively opened his good eye.

He made a mental note about where his books could be retrieved from the second floor fire escape, but thought better of knocking on a stranger's door in his present condition. Pulling a pencil from his pocket, he scrawled a note and his phone number on the back of an advertising flyer, waited for one of the building's occupants to enter, and slipping in behind her, climbed the stairs to slide a note under the door of the apartment that faced the front of the building. *I sure hope I get those back.*

Taking a last breath of heated air from the apartment building's warm lobby, he entered the foyer, opened the outer door, and continued down the street, shuffling his feet and looking down so his swollen face would be less noticeable to passers-by.

That's when he caught a glimpse of it – a greenish paper corner protruding from the snow. He reached down and retrieved a folded one-hundred-dollar bill: one hundred freaking miraculous American dollars – and not one of those phony advertising, "ha-ha-made-you-look-piss-you-off" hundred-dollar bills. This was "legal tender for all debts public and private." He slipped the bill into his jacket pocket and shook his head.

Jefferson stepped lightly despite his sore side and painful eye. If his "enlightened" classmates hadn't beaten him, he probably wouldn't have been looking down. He would have missed that tiny paper in the snow.

What a wonderful irony – poetic justice. He'd already concocted a long list of diabolical revenge fantasies – violent acts he'd inflict upon his truth-averse colleagues – but this unexpected boon inspired an idea. They'd be *expecting* some retaliation from him. He'd overlook what they'd done and let them look over their shoulders for a while – just let those poor stooges wonder when the never-to-happen strike would come. He chuckled and sauntered on, pleased with himself for having discovered his "revenge without revenge" strategy.

Snow fell and stung his cheeks. An icy wind blasted across the sidewalk from an adjacent alley. He zipped his jacket up tight and when the gust subsided, he noticed a figure in the shadows huddled behind a cluster of garbage cans – a shivering woman who had wrapped herself in newspapers to insulate herself from the cold.

Jefferson knew the temperature would continue to drop. He approached the woman. "Miss, take my jacket."

The woman looked at him through grateful tears. "But son, you..."

"I'm almost home," he said. "I'm not going to freeze before I get there. You keep warm and safe tonight."

Jefferson helped the woman slide her arms into the sleeves and pulled up the zipper. "Thank you, young man. You're my Christmas miracle."

"No," said Jefferson. "I'm just doing what's right."

Jefferson nodded and hurried the last few blocks home. He wanted to get there before he got uncomfortably cold, but mostly he didn't think it would be right to be there when the woman looked through his jacket pockets. That just wasn't how Santa worked.

High school sketch, circa 1980

Breathing Underwater

July, 1989

DIVING EVERY DAY, I grow accustomed to holding my breath. I don't know exactly how long I can stay down but the anxious feeling of running out of air simply disappears one day. I swim along the bottom of the reef, hunting under rocks and ledges. *Haven't I been down a while?* I swim some more, looking for the telltale antennae of spiny lobster protruding from hollows in the coral. *I really should go back up and take a breath.* I'm more nervous about being this comfortable staying down this long. I swim around some more and then, because it seems like a wise idea, I ascend, take a breath and return to the bottom.

"How ya comin' along, Dave?" John's voice crackles over the radio.

"Coming up on Man-O-War, but I can't see the entrance. Over."

"Keep on sailing. You can't miss it. Over."

I round Sandy Cay and Garden Cay, two small islets guarding Man-O-War's entrance channel. Man-O-War still looks like nothing but trees and coral. "I'll take your word for it. Over."

Over millennia, the waves have deeply undercut Man-O-War's rocky shoreline. The island sings strangely as the sea slaps metallically under the coral shelf.

It's calm in the lee of the island, a good place to take my sails down. I start my engine and continue on.

I still can't see a harbour entrance.

The bow of a boat emerges from the coral and scrub jungle shoreline. It's the Man-O-War ferry bound for Marsh Harbour. Good thing I wasn't in the channel – I'd have been run down – but now I know the way.

Inside is a different world. High hills rise before me. Prim white houses poke through the hardwood trees. Wooden docks line the shore of a secret lagoon, sheltered from high winds and surf. A fleet of tidy sailboats sleeps on moorings.

Just inside the entrance lies *Journeyman*, a classic double-ender.[5] Looking like the featured exhibit in a wooden boat museum, her hull is a symphony of varnish. A traditional, lapstraked[6] dinghy sits capsized on her cabin top under a sun awning. She's the most beautiful boat I've ever seen. *Now there's a boat I'd love to sail!*

Motoring east through the moored boats, I leave the shoal inside the entrance to starboard. There are no Dinner Key derelicts here. All these boats are solid enough to have made it across the Gulf Stream and on across the Bahama Banks against the trade winds. Today, I join them.

The unmistakable white-tipped masts of *Zebra Dun* appear. John stands shirtless on deck wearing zebra-striped sweat pants, hanging on to the shrouds. "Grab yourself that empty spot right over there," he calls, pointing to a place with some swinging room a hundred feet from his schooner.

I set my first anchor from the foredeck, fall back downwind and row a second hook out in the dinghy. After adjusting the rodes to position *Blue Monk* at a comfortable proximity to her new neighbors, I paddle over to the schooner.

True to his word, John has dinner simmering on the stove. Kipling, the ship's cat, comes out of hiding to rub her head against my hand. John smiles, then fixes me with his gaze, suggesting the importance of what he is about to impart. "You have arrived at a very special time in a very special place. I can't explain it but there's some sort of energy vortex here. Be careful what you ask for; you really *will* get it. This is a magic place." He doesn't elaborate further. "You'll see for yourself soon enough," he says after a reflective pause. "Here's your plate. Welcome to the Vortex."

After years of dreaming, months of preparation, a queasy passage across the Gulf Stream and a hard week of sailing to windward, I'm here – *somewhere.* I have time on my hands – lots of time. I practice guitar. I read a book every day. Coral heads lie just off the beach on the other side of the island. A short hike through the hardwood hammock[7] takes me to where I can swim out to them to hunt for fish and lobster. Sometimes, friends with motor dinghies offer a ride to the big barrier reef a mile offshore to stalk hogfish and grouper and lobster among the corals.

I dive on the wreck of the *Adirondack,* a Civil War ship sunk on the reef in 1862. Old boilers, engine parts, and cannon lie strewn among the corals. A shimmering paisley peacock flounder undulates over a brain coral. Thousands of tiny, silvery fish flash in the sun, moving in unison as if controlled by a single will.

In the cut between the west side of Man-O-War Cay and the Fowl Cays, I don my dive mask, lean over and poke my head underwater. Conch[8] amble slowly across the shallow bottom. They're small but hopefully big enough to make dinner of. By the time I kick my way to the sea floor, I'm completely out of breath. The water is at least fifty feet deep, but so clear I would never have guessed. The conch aren't small – they're *huge.* Many who have been here longer than me can make this dive easily, but I'm barely able. With one of the head-sized, weed-covered shells in each hand, I kick off the bottom, struggling to the surface, barely mastering my body's overpowering urge to inhale.

Hunting for my supper is new to me. I don't like killing things, even fish, but I learn to do it with conviction. It's worse to wound a fish and have it swim away to die slowly. I wait for a clean shot, pull back as far as I can on the rubber tubing that launches the pole spear through my hands, and aim carefully. Once I skewer enough food for dinner, I often linger on the reef to enjoy the scenery, but the hunt is over; I'm a guest here. Fish and other sea creatures brought home to the galley are always thanked and apologized to. I've never been fond of superstition or ritual but there are predators in the ocean who would just as happily have *me* for dinner. I feel spontaneously grateful every time I am privileged to be the eater, and not the eatee.

Pizza with lobster on it emerges from John's oven.

I cook lobster omelets for breakfast.

I confess to John I'm growing tired of the stuff. He feels the same way but we can only laugh at ourselves – two penniless boat bums growing weary of the food of the rich.

"Be careful what you wish for," John repeats with a laugh.

I usually take to my bunk not long after sundown. I rise at first light, in sync with the rhythm of the earth. Tonight, before retiring, I put a piece of fish on a hook and drop it in the water beside *Blue Monk*, wrapping the fishing line around the starboard cockpit winch. In the middle of the night, the clicking of the winch pall awakens me. A mutton snapper fights at the end my line – a big one – more than John and I could ever eat before it would spoil in our unrefrigerated galleys, but wasting a bounty like this would be an unacceptable affront. In the morning, I clean the snapper and then row around Man-O-War anchorage distributing baggies of fresh fish to my neighbors.

In the afternoons, I row into town to the tiny Man-O-War post office to ask pretty young Charmaine Albury if there's any mail for me. When I'm not inclined to row, I tie my dinghy at the Lee's private dock – they don't mind me landing there – to hike the Queen's Highway through the hardwood hammock up the spine of the island into the settlement. Near the far end of the southeastern harbour where we're anchored, the Queen's Highway is nothing more than a simple, unpaved footpath through the jungle. Terrestrial scents of gumelemi, seagrape, and poisonwood trees blend with sea smells as the breeze filters through the tropical woods. Ambient, crashing surf on the rocks beyond the trees accompanies the rhythm of my feet. I carry my shoes until my feet grow uncomfortable; they aren't tough enough yet to handle the entire journey.

A paved road joins the coral path at the edge of town. Tidy pastel houses of wood or cinderblock sit in yards lined with conch shells. Some are festooned with fishing floats. A row of whale vertebrae lines a front fence. The hardware store sits near the boatyard where the Albury family still builds boats by hand, the way they have for generations. A few small grocery stores stand among Man-O-War's colonial houses, churches, marinas and the schoolhouse. Down a short side street, overlooking the ocean, stands the world's most exquisite baseball field. In view of third base, past a strip of sandy beach, the surf explodes into spray against the rocks. I rest on a log bench here at the edge of the field before turning back. To the north, the Atlantic is turquoise, dappled with coral heads and cloud shadows out to a white strip where breakers collide with the reef. Beyond the breakers, the bottom drops off into a band of deep blue beneath the horizon.

The beach is deserted. Today I'll walk back along the shoreline and cut back to the Queen's highway through the woods farther down.

I'm offered a small varnishing job – strictly under the table – foreigners aren't allowed to work here – but it puts a hundred dollars in my pocket. That should cover fresh vegetables and laundry expenses for another six weeks.

In spite of living on so little, I have never lived so well, but a lingering restlessness follows me. Old habits of arranging my day to confront a list of obligations don't fade easily. My life has been work, work, work, schedule, schedule, schedule. Now, I can do anything I want, any time I want – in spite of the nagging feeling I'm neglecting something. I'm used to laboring all week for a paycheck that barely keeps up with expenses. Here, three days of work carries me for months.

Is it *acceptable* to live like this?

Can life be *this* easy?

"The human being," declares John Nation, "is the only animal on planet earth not in captivity that doesn't do exactly what it wants to do."

I have some money in my pocket. John's earned some, too. I suggest a change of pace, a run to Marsh Harbour to restock our pantries at a big grocery store. It's time for a supply run and maybe even a splurge at a local restaurant. Late Saturday afternoon, we hoist sails and haul anchors. Our two boats reach together across the Sea of Abaco into the falling sun.

Sunday morning is filled with island sounds.

A rooster crows.

Somewhere in town, a big diesel generator sputters and begins to drone.

A few dinghies and some larger speedboats zoom about the harbour.

A big ketch arrives and drops anchor.

Two other cruising yachts leave with a rattle of anchor chains.

A short walk up the hill, across the main road, past the telephone company and the liquor store takes us to the Saint Frances de Sales Catholic Mission, a small cinderblock building next to which a tent has been erected over a concrete foundation – a temporary substitute for the wooden sanctuary that burned the year before.

Beneath the canopy, Marsh Harbour's Haitian community gathers for Sunday mass.

"Don't worry," John encourages. "I'm not a Catholic either, but you don't want to miss this. Catholics don't really care if you're Catholic or not; that's one of the things I like about 'em."

The morning is hot, still, and humid. Mosquitoes stalk unprotected ankles above the wet grass. People sweat, wipe dripping foreheads, fan themselves and shuffle on their feet. These humble refugees have come in their finest clothing to offer gratitude for deliverance into a land of new hope. No strangers to the tropical heat, the spirited worshipers refuse to acknowledge it. Higher priorities are in play. The air is festive.

An electric guitar squawks through a tinny amplifier as its player makes a futile attempt to tune it. Random beats sound on a drum. The priest steps up to the lectern at the front of the tent. The chatter of the crowd quickly dies away.

After a few words in Creole, the guitar and drums begin. The congregation rises to sing *Papa Nou* (Our Father). We are among the few light-skinned attendees, but we are welcomed. We join hands with the worshipers in the back of the open-sided tent and sing along as best we can.

After the crowd disperses, John introduces me to a thin, fiftyish woman. "Meet Sister Eleanor, an old friend from my last Abaco trip. She's in charge of the mission school."

Sister Eleanor is nothing like what I expect a nun to be. After working with inner city kids in New York, she's tough, but also kind and humorous and witty. We're welcomed and invited to have lunch with the current crop of recent college graduates who have volunteered to teach at the mission school. They seek experience to enhance their résumés – to help them find jobs when they return to their faraway homes on the other side of the Gulf Stream.

I raise an eyebrow at John and question him telepathically. *You mean this place even comes with a house full of twenty-two-year old girls?*

My friend nods discreetly and smiles.

Gathering around a wooden table before a plate full of peanut butter sandwiches and a pitcher of 'bug juice,' we link our little fingers together and close our eyes.

"Terry, you say grace," says Sister Eleanor.

"Rub-a-dub-dub. Thanks for the grub," chants Terry. After a brief pause, she opens her eyes and continues, "Amen. Everybody dig in."

Man-O-War is only an hour's sail away.

I'm in no rush to sail back.

John strings a hammock between his two masts under a large canvas awning.

The breeze fills in.

"Do you mind if I…?"

"Not at all," says John. "Crawl in there and take a nap. Enjoy yourself."

I recall nothing of the next three days. I remain ensconced in a cotton chrysalis, suspended between two spruce masts. If I ate, used the toilet, or got out of the hammock even once during that time, I have no recollection of it.

The restlessness disappears.

Is it *acceptable* to live any way else?

I am happy here.

Now.

"I'm ready to sail back over to Man-O-War," I announce to John.

I want to hike barefoot down the Queen's Highway.

The soles of my feet are tough as leather.

I want to dive for conch in Man-O-War cut.

I can stay down forever.

— *The Blue Monk*, 2016

High school sketch, circa 1980

The Garden Slug

1981

There are some creatures 'pon this earth
I would not care to hug
Among them I feel I must include
The common garden slug

It moves its solitary foot
Along a trail of slime
And covers little distance
In a long amount of time

I know not hot to classify
This animal so odd
My only guess would be to call the thing
A "monopod"

It bears no bulky snail's shell
No home upon its back
Preferring more mobility
To protection from attack

So please don't harm the garden slug
Don't mash it into paste
Or flick its little eyestalks off
For that would be a waste

Have respect for the garden slug
In its defenseless state
Let not its presence make you feel
Offended or irate

And ponder you this verse
And all the meaning it entails
And join me in my reverence
For this most bizarre of snails

Master and Commander

Stocking Island, Georgetown, Exuma 1981

SOME TIME AFTER TEN O'CLOCK, Bruce awoke. Light streamed through a porthole next to his bunk, and a tiny voice reminded him he should get around to polishing its bronze bezel before it took on too much more of a greenish patina. He stared for a minute at the wood grain of the teak ceiling adjacent to his bunk, set his empty wine bottle back upright, and sampled a corn chip from an open bag to confirm his unarticulated suspicion that it and its siblings had gone stale during the night. He stretched, and then clasped the tiny remainder of last night's joint in a pair of toenail clippers so he could finish it off without burning his lips. The annoying bronze-polishing voice forgot to nag him again.

He stumbled to the head,[9] performed his morning ablutions, and grabbed fists full of breakfast from a box of dry corn flakes.

Climbing the companionway ladder, he stopped half way up, put his elbows on the bridge deck, and looked around at the anchorage.

Cool trimaran over there.... Cute girl on board, too.

He felt a pang of boredom, but then reminded himself he was the professional captain of the *Ne Plus Ultra*, charged with great responsibility and paid – modestly perhaps, but still paid – to live on a yacht in exotic, tropical locales. Bruce cultivated his moment of self-importance, and then, feeling he should do something definitively nautical and responsible to validate his sense of duty and importance, he continued his climb to the cockpit, now with slightly more swagger to his movements. He started the engine.

Ne Plus Ultra was a yawl of 1920s vintage that had been lovingly and expensively restored and modernized. She glowed with twelve coats of fine varnish on her wooden hull, and her sitka spruce masts and booms sported the same high-gloss finish with their tips painted white in the traditional fashion. Ratlines neatly tied to the lower shrouds made a rope-runged ladder up to the point where a topmast[10] was affixed to the main mast, enhancing her classic appearance. The stern narrowed almost to a point where a tiny, varnished transom had room only for the vessel's initials, rendered in gold leaf as a Victorian "NPE" monogram that might have graced an antique pocket watch case. A cream-colored sheer stripe accented the vessel's feminine curves and provided a background for her full name to be emblazoned, again in gold leaf, just aft of the foredeck on each side of the bow. A maroon drop shadow accented the gold typography, and a long, varnished bowsprit,[11] enshrouded with black chains provided a perch for a traditional fisherman's anchor. A patch or two of reddish-brown tanbark sail canvas peeked from beneath her cream sail covers.

No doubt she was a beauty, and Bruce, standing in her cockpit in a pair of cutoff denim shorts with hands behind his head, listened to the water splashing from the engine's cooling exhaust and surveyed his kingdom. The engine came to temperature and Bruce reduced the idle speed slightly. Today would be a good day to do captain-like activities, though thoughts of polishing bronze or varnishing the dinette table offered little reinforcement to his sense of authority. It dawned on him there was only a very modest wind, and a show of casually moving the boat to the other side of the anchorage would not be an inappropriate exercise of his right and privilege as the vessel's master.

Bruce stuffed another handful of cornflakes into his mouth, scattering a few on the cockpit sole, and strode up to the foredeck.

The anchor lines were wrapped around each other several times as he'd sat here at Stocking island through three northers with the wind clocking around each time. The breeze was now such that one line was slack while the *Ultra* hung on the other. Pulling the last fifty feet of line through one of the hawsepipes in the foredeck, he coiled up the line, uncleated the slack rode and, placing his feet on the bowsprit shrouds, made his way out past the spare anchor to where the lines came over the bronze rollers and twisted together under the bobstay.

For a moment, Bruce fumbled around with the lines and then, momentarily losing his balance, grabbed for the bowsprit as he dropped the coil of line into the water.

He looked around. *Nobody watching. Good.*

The dropped line was still looped around the taught line; it would be easy to retrieve it. He began to make his way back to the deck where a boathook was tied to the forward shrouds, but then he looked at the line coiled loosely on the sea bottom and thought it would be easier to jump in and pull the slack line over the taught one from down in the water.

The water was refreshing. Bruce floated for a moment, wishing he'd remembered to bring some salt water soap. He had, of course, also neglected to lower the boarding ladder, but after untwisting the line, he swam aft to where a prim, white lapstraked dinghy was tied next to the cockpit, it's varnished interior glowing with the warmth of antique wood and shimmering with the reflections of the Bahamian sky. Struggling into it, he incurred only minor scrapes to his belly, and introduced only twenty gallons or so of sea water into its interior.

Let that wood soak a bit. The salt water is good for it.

Leaving the dinghy with the water in its bilge, he made his way back forward along the port side to the foredeck, retracing his steps once after neglecting to run the end of the anchor line he was carrying outside the shrouds. He tied the line off at its bitter end, let the slack coils of line settle to the sandy bottom, and then began pulling in the remaining anchor from which hung the *Ne Plus Ultra*.

After a minute, he tired and cleated off the line. He'd be damned if he knew where the windlass handle had gone off to. There was just enough breeze to make hauling the vessel against it a chore, and now that he'd lost his momentum, he'd have to start again. He stood on the deck catching his breath with his hands on his knees, a posture that accentuated the beer and junk food-induced extra thirty pounds on his stomach.

"Check out this guy over there," said Hanns. "Everything he touches turns to shit."

Yvonne chuckled and positioned herself in *Chaos's* cockpit at such an angle that it wouldn't be obvious she was watching the spectacle aboard the *Ne Plus Ultra* a hundred feet way.

Spying his audience despite their efforts to be discreet, Bruce waved at his neighbors, and resolved to put on a show of competent and capable boat handling commensurate with the appearance and quality of the vessel in his charge.

It occurred to him the engine was already running, and at low speed, it might provide a gentle push that would make a simple matter of bringing the boat to the windward anchor. Returning to the cockpit, he put the engine in gear and then stationed himself on the bow where, as the boat idled forward, he was able to comfortably reel in the line at a speed that allowed him to coil it neatly on deck. The chain followed, and Bruce heaped it in the center of the coil before cleating it off and allowing the momentum of the boat to break loose the forty-pound plough anchor that, with some strain, he was able to haul up to the bowsprit.

Breathing hard from exertion, he paused to celebrate his success.

The engine stopped with a "clunk."

"Dammit!"

The leeward anchor line now became taught and arrested the vessel's forward motion. His ship sat facing the wind for a moment, as if undecided about what to do next, and then slowly turned sideways and began to fall back downwind.

Yvonne looked at Hanns. "That anchor line's wrapped around his propeller isn't it?"

"Sure as shit. Do you think he'll have the sense to toss that anchor back after he just worked so hard to wrestle it up?"

Bruce leaped awkwardly aft to the cockpit, put the engine in neutral, started the diesel again, and popped it into gear.

It died with an immediate mechanical sound that resonated through the *Ultra*'s wooden topsides.

Hanns stood up in the cockpit. "He's about to do the unthinkable."

"Which is…?"

Bruce returned the engine to neutral, restarted it and pushed the throttle all the way forward. A cloud of smoke issued from the exhaust just under the transom; the scream of the tortured machine fractured the tranquility of the clear morning.

With a posture full of resolve and panic, he took the gear shift handle in his fist and slammed it forward.

The roar of the engine transitioned to silence with a pounding and impactful percussion, made oddly musical by the wooden hull from which it emanated, as if a missile had struck a marimba factory. Smoke now rose gently through the companionway from inside the cabin of the *Ne Plus Ultra*, and Bruce leaned against the binnacle[12] in the cockpit, defeated.

"Yvonne, if you'll let out an extra seventy-five feet or so of line on that starboard anchor, we can give our drifting neighbor over there a little passing room. I'll buzz over in the dinghy and see if I can't help prevent him from doing anything else that might aspire to seamanship."

The *Ne Plus Ultra* drifted sideways over her remaining submerged anchor to the edge of the harbor where she settled stern-to the wind, hanging from her propeller a mere thirty feet from the beach.

– *Waves,* 2011

Water

"WATER," said Carl Jung, "is the commonest symbol for the unconscious." In these islands, the sea is clear; the bottom is visible. In a realm so potent with symbolism, water bends perspective as readily as light, inspiring visions powerful, moving and transcendent.

Cathy's Island

I anchor at Powell Cay, a less-traveled island northwest of Green Turtle. Uninhabited, the island is serenely quiet with beaches void of human footprints and a grove of tall, wild coconut palms. On the lee side, dramatic coral cliffs shelter tropicbirds nesting in their season. Affixed to the rocks near the anchorage is a small, bronze plaque – "Cathy Swedenborg Loved This Island" – a shrine to a young woman who died here with her boyfriend in 1979 when their boat burned. Her epitaph is unconcerned with what was lost. Instead, it connects her forever to this special place she found and appreciated, and to her enduring suggestion that I might love it, too.

Late at night, I awaken and step into the cockpit. Unadulterated by urban incandescence, untinted by the azure hue of day, the nocturnal world projects its magic for those fortunate to bear witness.

The moon is high and bright; the white sand bottom illuminated like a stadium; the lunar light brilliant enough to read by.

I step astern, grabbing the backstay for support.

A diamond shape moves in the water below me.

And another.

Giant Atlantic Stingrays glide over the bottom: dozens of them. Their dark forms undulate, slow and graceful against brilliant, subaquatic sand; an Escher woodcut brought to life; a moving tapestry of figure and ground; a dream landscape.

Such sights may be common. Stingrays may congregate here regularly on moonlit nights – or perhaps – maybe only once – tonight. It doesn't matter; I am blessed to witness a secret world of shadows and light.

Cathy Swedenborg loved this island.

I understand.

Swimming in the Light

At night, especially during summers when the ocean is warm, the sea is alive with bioluminescence. Microscopic creatures glow firefly-green where the water is agitated. On a dark night, swimming in Neptune's domain is an unnatural experience; my body emanates sparkling fire; propellers leave trails of light; swirls of green remain where oars are withdrawn from the water.

Tonight, in the lagoon at Man-O-War Cay, the phosphorescent magic is particularly potent. On awakening, I ascend to the cockpit to marvel at the stars above the silhouettes of the jungle-covered hills that protect this anchorage from ocean swells.

The night is quiet and still.

I hear the sea crashing against the rocks on the far side of the island.

Something breathes deeply – something close – a quick exhalation followed by an inward breath.

Ripples spread across placid water.

A glowing green dolphin glides below the anchored boats, leaving a phosphorescent contrail behind her. I watch in rapture as she crisscrosses the lagoon. Periodically, she surfaces to breathe among the sleeping vessels. Man-O-War is a small place, and no bountiful fishing ground compared to the barrier reef thriving with life a short mile away. Why would she even be here if not to dance in the light?

Dolphins frequently venture into shallow anchorages to swim among our boats. How must we appear to them? With their sophisticated hearing and echolocation systems, they can surely observe us in our strange wood and fiberglass nests. I wonder what they think, these creatures who live in the sea yet breathe air, of those who live in the sky yet sleep beneath the water.

Clarity

Daylight skies are blue. Sunlight is yellow or orange at dawn and dusk, and pure white at noon. Under these influences, the natural hues of the diurnal landscape are a feast of color, but the nocturnal realm is illuminated by no such chromatic vibrancy. Uncolored by the pastels of daytime illumination, Bahamian water untouched by sunlight takes on even more remarkable clarity. White light from stars and the bleached surface of the lifeless moon render the world of night a sonata of contrasted silvers and blacks. Brilliant reflections dance on shimmering seas, yet are subject to manipulation by changes in viewing angle. Each observer perceives a landscape uniquely decorated by his own proximity to the light.

With the moon approaching the horizon, *Blue Monk* lies at anchor with a few other boats near Great Guana Cay. As I row, neither the tiniest breath of wind nor the faintest eddy of tidal flow disturbs the surface.

The water is transparent as air.

I am not rowing; I am *flying*.

The boundary between air and sea is indistinguishable. Ribbons of reflected light curl from my bow, dissipating into nothing as I glide across the water. Like my dinghy, our anchored boats hover rather than float over shadows undisturbed by the refractive effects of moving waves. Adrift in the atmosphere above dangling anchor lines clearly visible in the sand below, my senses warn me to avoid falling even as logic assures me the invisible water still holds me up. How odd, magical, and surreal to find such clarity in darkness.

Blue Holes

Little Harbour is the last stop on Great Abaco before the ninety-mile long island elbows southward into bottomless abyss. Beyond the small reef where the chain of out-islands ends, the North Atlantic embraces the island's coast directly. Little Harbour is a world of its own with a protected lagoon, caves full of bats to explore, an old lighthouse on a sea cliff stationed above a place where ocean waves detonate into foam against the rocks below, and a bronze foundry set up by sculptor Randolph Johnston who settled here in the 1950s. West of Little Harbour lies the Bight of Old Robinson, a shallow, oval bay rimmed by rings of coral. John Nation suggests it might be an astrobleme – a scar from an ancient meteorite strike. We snorkel among the rocky ridges at the perimeter, hunting for fish and lobster.

While swimming across the shallow sea floor, I encounter a yawning cavern – a blue hole – a forty-foot wide, infinitely deep subterranean passageway connected in some distant place to the ocean.

Richard, a French sailor with a steel boat joins us today. Lost overboard on the Bahama Banks in a storm a year before, he swam for days before dragging himself up on a desolate rock at the edge of the Gulf Stream. Thirsty and sunburned, he was rescued by a passing yachtsman while his girlfriend waited, despondent, in Bimini, having reluctantly given up the search for lack of fuel and hope. Upon being reunited with him, she offered him anything she could afford to give. Today, he wears his chosen gift; a pair of freediving fins as long as your arm from fingertip to shoulder. He takes a deep breath before descending, then disappears into the eerie gloom below me.

Blue holes like these dot the Bahamas. A few, like one not far from Marsh Harbour, are landlocked and possibly of some utility; what goes into a blue hole stays in a blue hole. One can imagine the nature of countless furtive missions to the secret pond in the Abaco pines since the Lucaya Indians first inhabited this place centuries ago.

Depth

In the Bahamas, where the bottom is not visible, the water is deep – *really* deep. After passing through the cut in Little Harbour's reef before sundown, I sail overnight to make Nassau in the light of morning – daylight arrival being a prudent practice for calling anywhere in these shallow and poorly marked islands. About two thirds of the way between Little Harbour and New Providence Island, the chart shows a wide, conical depression in the ocean floor – 4,762 meters – almost three miles deep. Falling that distance from the sky to the ground would take eight minutes. Add water resistance to that descent and you have time to think while you sink. The pressure at the bottom is 473 times what it is at the surface and yet, living creatures inhabit that inky blackness. That world is better imagined than experienced but it inspires no less wonder.

I check my compass heading again, adjust course, and consider the thin fiberglass shell that contains only myself, my humble human effects, and enough air to buoy me high above the distant bottom.

Sailing here is as profound as staring into the Milky Way.

Water is a symbol of the unconscious. Floating over miles of blackness, riding the invisible boundary between sky and sea, I traverse many planes. In the infinite depths of the ocean, I confront my own fathomless mystery. In clear shallows, what lies beneath the surface is both revealed and obscured by reflection. Travelers across an aqueous landscape of clear shallows, deep oceans, peaceful calms, explosive turbulence, vibrant color, and sparkling contrast encounter visions no less beautiful, moving and inspiring than any dream – visions illuminated by an inner force as powerful as the light of the stars.

– *The Blue Monk,* 2016

Ode to a Rainy Day After Day

2017

This rain keeps falling
Drizzling, dripping
Pattering upon my pane
Falling, falling
Ever falling
Gray and humid
Comes the rain

Days go past
Precipitation
Thrums and hums
And drums and numbs
I'm lost in aimless

Death of the Guitar

Cogitation
Reason to the rain succumbs

Drops assault the ground
Relentless
Days become a week
Eventless
Soporific
Moist and soggy
Saturated
Dull and doggy

Dank and dreary
Wet and smeary
Cold and clammy
This? Miami?
Where's the sun?
Christ! It's December!
Yet the rain
Keeps falling down

Ode to a Rainy Day After Day

Has it been a week already
That this rain's been falling steady?
Trickling on without improvement
For some wicked God's amusement
Show'ring on and on and on
Oh cease, I say
Anon, anon

Joints are creaky
And rheumatic
Water penetrates
My attic
Life's become
So stark and static
Think I'm going to
Build an ark

Lord, I hope the time is nearing
When the sun will be appearing
And the clouds commence to clearing

And the atmosphere stops drearing
But I must confess I'm fearing
That this rain
Will linger on
And on and on
And on and on

Chop Wood; Carry Water

STRIDER COLLECTED HIS GUEST'S DIRTY DISHES in a five-gallon bucket of seawater. Micky Tomm scrubbed the plates and cutlery and handed them to Strider who rinsed them lightly with fresh water. "Fresh water is not something that flows out of the tap like magic, here," explained Strider. In the U.S., you flip a switch or turn on a tap or flush a toilet; lights glow, hands get clean, and waste disappears – hocus-pocus. In the islands, we collect rainwater or buy it when we have to. Here you'd never throw away a *gallon* of fresh water every time you pee. And soon enough, Americans are going to find out that their story of the magic faucet doesn't hold water. A lot of folks are *not* going to be happy about that. The average American uses 80–100 gallons of water per day. That's almost the full capacity of *The Metaphor*'s tanks. The story that magic flows out of our pipes and walls is a seductive one, but it's dangerous, and because water and energy – especially energy – are *big business,* industries are capitalizing on that phony story to collect money while they destroy the planet."

"So how do we rewrite that story?" asked Doug. "We teach about conserving fresh water in junior high school, but I'm not sure we're changing minds."

"There's a famous Zen saying: 'Before enlightenment: chop wood; carry water. After enlightenment: chop wood; carry water.' It refers to the idea that life is full of mundane tasks, and that pursuit of a spiritual existence doesn't excuse you from getting your laundry done and washing between your toes. You don't get to sit around chanting with a robe on while the angels follow you around and wipe your bottom for you. But the problem, as I see it, is that nobody's chopping wood or carrying water *after or before* enlightenment because enlightenment flows out of their tap. Chop the wood yourself and you won't burn so many logs. Carry the water yourself and you won't use a gallon of it to rinse away a cup of pee.

"What you can do about it is exactly what you *are* doing about it. Live out in the world for a few days and sleep under the stars. Find out what so many people are insulated from. Take your newfound appreciation back to the land of clocks and calendars and encourage others to have the experience you're having.

"Another aphorism – it might be contemporary; it's attributed to a few sources, but it has the ring of an old Zen saying, and it might even be one: 'If you wear shoes, the whole earth is covered with leather.' How can we teach children to love the earth when we don't teach them what it feels like to walk barefoot in the grass?"

Strider wiped the last of the plates and rose from the galley. He ascended the first step of the companionway ladder and poked his head out into the fading Abaco dusk before returning below to address the happiness delegates. "We have a south wind," he explained, "which means we probably have a cold front coming. That in itself is probably not a big deal, but assuming we haven't missed our weather window, we want to hightail it out of here at first light, get around Whale Cay – which we can't do once the wind clocks around to the north and starts hissing and spitting – and get anchored up over at Marsh Harbour. If the weather gods find us worthy, maybe they'll bless us with enough time to get supplies at the big store there and then move on to Man-O-War Cay before the rain comes."

The captain surveyed the cabin. "Before we transition oh-so-appropriately from Zen sayings into tonight's assault on reality, let's get the gear stowed and the sail covers stripped off. If we do see any rough weather tomorrow, I don't want stuff crashing all over the boat."

The happiness delegates busied themselves tidying up for a few minutes and then reconvened on deck.

"How do you know there's a cold front coming," asked Kaitlin, "and at the risk of sounding ignorant, what *is* a cold front?"

Strider smiled and fingered the brim of his hat. "I'll give you the short version: The wind in this part of the world blows slightly south of east most of the time. But an approaching weather system – in this case, a bubble of cold air moving down from the Arctic – a 'cold front' – can affect the local wind direction before it actually gets here. Think of it as a 'weather shadow.' When the wind moves past southeast, it will most likely clock all the way around to the north and then back around to the southeast once the front has blown through.

"I'm sure Lenore could tell us all about the Coriolis effect and other interesting physical properties that affect the weather…"

Lenore nodded.

"…but let's skip the science lesson and plug that back into the world of 'things the average homeowner doesn't pay much attention to.' If you take off those leather shoes, the earth will talk to you in all sorts of wonderful ways. When you tune into it and listen, you gain a different appreciation for it."

Walter raised a wine glass. "I'm going to play the skeptic again."

"Please do," encouraged Strider. "If no one questions, it usually means no one is listening – which usually means I'm ranting about something."

"I'm all good with your 'tune into the earth' message; I get that – but what's the relationship between that and connection and engagement and happiness?

I'm not challenging what you're saying, but I'm challenging you to keep it on-message."

"Good," said Strider. "Knowing me, that's always a wise idea."

"If there's *one* thing we *should* all be able to connect over, it's the idea that we have a common interest in caring for the planet that sustains us. When we live in a way that puts us in touch with what the wind says, when we engage with the seasons in a way that runs deeper than choosing between the heater and the air-conditioner, when we learn to time the tides so we can cross the shallows when the water is high, when we watch the stars instead of the ceiling tiles, the earth becomes a *character* in our shared story. Technology is wonderful – and how many of us would even be here if it weren't for antibiotics? – but when I see people walking down a beautiful beach and they're staring at their stupidphones, I want to shake them and wake them up.

"Ten thousand years ago, humans were still living in caves and hunting mammoths. In geological or evolutionary terms, that's a blink of an eye. Now we're flying around in airplanes and sending people to the moon and navigating with satellites and curing cancer and making microchips and talking to friends on the other side of the world. That's all wonderful, but we've grown too fast; our stories – including some important ones – have been left behind. Our psychic story writers can't keep up.

"Walter, you've been connecting to and engaging with the earth on a different level since you arrived in these islands three days ago. You've had to conserve fresh water and use kerosene lanterns to read by and travel to and from shore with a rowing dinghy, but you've seen the reef and the stars and used the wind to push you from one island to another. What do you think?"

Walter closed his eyes. "It's all magnificent. It's beyond words. It's…"

"So when you get back to your home and work – to your so-called 'real life,' how will you use this experience to enhance the way you connect and engage with audiences at your speeches? Hasn't this journey been one big exercise in connection and engagement?"

"I'm not sure. That's why I asked…"

"And that's the answer; I wish I had a better one for you. Too many people don't speak 'Earth.' Their stories are missing a vitally important character. Try starting a story with, 'I stuck my head out the hatch the other day and noticed the wind had gone south.'" It'll be crickets and tumbleweeds for sure – no applause for you.

"Our culture is losing stories; its smile looks like mine." Strider showed off his missing front tooth. "You can't use the wind and the tide and the ways the birds are behaving to connect with people – but you *should* be able to.

"Audrey, you're a psychologist. You deal with the effects of missing stories all day."

"What do you mean?"

"Men and women see the world differently. How many times have you taught couples how to listen and respond in each other's gender language? A woman marries a man thinking he'll change; a man marries a woman thinking she won't. Why do couples get together and struggle to harmonize their stories? Why isn't conflict resolution a required class for fourth, seventh, and eleventh graders? Why is Sex Education all about body parts?"

Audrey shrugged.

"For all our technology and the millions of books we've published, you still have to spend thousands of dollars to attend a workshop if you want to discover the 'secrets to happiness.' That's because the tapestry of stories that makes up our society is full of holes. That drafty blanket isn't keeping us warm anymore."

Walter pushed harder. "All good stuff, Strider, but I don't think you answered my question. You've given me ways I *should* be able to connect and engage but can't. How do I turn this around and use it?"

Strider raised an index finger and looked at his guests. "Write the missing stories," he said. "Find the gaps and fill them in. Steal some people's shoes. Turn off their main breakers and shut off their water. Kidnap them and take them out to sea or deep into the woods. Write the missing chapters in the *homo sapiens* instruction manual."

"That's a tall order," said Micky Tomm.

"Of course it is," replied Strider, "but that's what leaders and happy people do. Chop wood; carry water."

— *The Story Story,* 2018

Duende

TINO TOOK A DEEP BREATH, stretched his hands and cracked his knuckles before quietly flipping open the latches of the guitar case. Almost inaudibly, he tuned his instrument, taking care to integrate the sound of the tuning rhythmically and melodically into the music, and then after another short pause to listen, he closed his eyes and began to play.

A smile slowly appeared on the boy's face as he sensed Tino's ability and presence. He offered a phrase to Tino who immediately improvised a musical response. El Dedo answered and then, anticipating Tino's phrase, followed with a perfect harmony line beneath it. The second guitarist stopped playing so he could listen. The fire crackled as something collapsed inside the barrel and a torrent of sparks flew up into the darkness. Tino and the boy chased each other, alternately testing each other and providing musical support for one another's melodic excursions, exploring the boundaries of technique and time, whispering, shouting, making love, waging war, praying over, damning, and transporting all who listened to a world beyond matter and energy. The percussionist cried out unconsciously from his trance.

For an eternal hour or more, the two guitarists cavorted. The boy broke a string and kept playing. Almost immediately after, one of Tino's strings gave way but the dance continued. Finally, with a woody twang, another string popped on Tino's guitar and the music collapsed into laughter.

Tino embraced the boy like an old friend, and bowed to him. *"Bravo, amigo. Maravilloso!"*

Wordlessly, the boy smiled and gracefully bowed his head in return. Hanns's eyes sparkled in the firelight, and Kalimba leaned back contentedly in his chair, his arms crossed and his feet propped up on an old milk crate.

While Tino and the boy restrung and retuned, a few more men with guitars came to sit by the fire. Another man tossed some boards into the barrel and the flames climbed high once again, revealing the faces and instruments of the ring of musicians in orange contrast to the blackness of the night. One of the guitarists started a *bulería.* A man appeared out of the shadows to sing an interpretation of a Lorca poem. A dark woman undulated in a long white skirt and a simple black tube top before the orange light as the music rose, the flames revealing the delicate shape of her lithe figure through the cotton gauze. The players shouted back and forth to encourage one another until a nod brought the performance to a perfectly coordinated finish that froze the dancer, her anguished face looking downward, two fingers pressed to her brow as if in mourning.

– *The Dance,* 2009

High school sketch, circa 1980

The Master

2017

Master

I wish to become enlightened

But first
How do I know
You are really a master?

It does not matter

How do you know
You are not
Already enlightened?

High school sketch, circa 1980

Gift Horse

Government Docks, San Juan Puerto Rico, March, 1978

After thanking the taxi driver, Werner, Raquel, and Hanns walked down the pier, boarded a rust-streaked ship, and descended a creaky metal stairway into the cargo hold. The hum of an electric pump accompanied a watery sound from under the floorboards, many of which were soggy plywood replacements for decks that had long since rusted through. Two flickering yellow lights illuminated a dreary space, though the green steel bulkheads displayed empty receptacles for at least four more bulbs.

Hanns shrugged. "She's not pretty but if she'll stay afloat, she'll do the job. At sixty-five feet, you won't find anything smaller that still qualifies as a bona fide cargo boat. She doesn't draw too much, she's not made of wood, and she's small enough to handle like a yacht. We don't need a full-fledged ship on our hands."

"She lists to one side," observed Werner.

"I'm wondering about that, myself. I can't figure out why. *Something's* off-balance." Hanns smiled. "Maybe the starboard side has lost more metal to rust?"

Turning the wheel lock on the heptangular[13] door to the engine room, Hanns fumbled for a light switch. Finding none, he switched on his flashlight and laughed. "Now *this* is a museum piece – an original one-cylinder diesel – probably about fifty horsepower."

Raquel grabbed his arm. "Do you think she'll run?"

"The wonderful thing about these engines is they don't have many parts to break. If this motor's not frozen – and it appears to be the only part of this boat anyone cared about for the past thirty years – it should run forever." Hanns pulled the oil dipstick and shined his light on it. "See? Pure golden honey."

Werner stared at the machine critically. "I don't know much about engines, but fifty horsepower doesn't seem like a lot."

"You're right, but she's not built for speed; she's built for reliability and torque. She's got a big, low-pitched prop. If she were an automobile, she'd make a terrible race car but she'd make a wonderful tractor. Boats like this were built to shuttle sardines between New England fishing boats and processing plants on shore, probably during the late forties after the war. She's a relic from the early days of factory fishing, back when they first decided the oceans were a resource to mine without limits twenty-four hours a day. She was designed to haul heavy loads in heavy seas. I'm sure her salty cargo contributed to all the rust eating her today. I'm liking the big new aluminum fuel tank, though. Her previous owners obviously wanted long range and clean diesel."

"But is she safe?"

"She's been floating here at the dock for a year, though I imagine not without the help of a few pumps. She does have an eight-man life raft with a recent inspection certificate. That mitigates a certain amount of risk."

"I wonder," said Werner, "how an old boat like this winds up in a government auction in San Juan, Puerto Rico."

"Easy; she's a perfect drug boat. She's got a hull with so many shades of peeling green paint, she's almost camouflaged. Someone installed a big fuel tank for long range and she can hold several tons of cargo. I imagine most of these boats came here the same way; they're all DEA[14] seizures."

"Aren't you worried a doper will outbid us on her?"

"I suspect the drugrunners don't want the government to know when they buy a boat like this; they can buy vessels from plenty of other sources. Most of the bidders will be people looking for deals on speedboats and sport fishermen. Possibly, a few speculators might want to put a new interior in a stripped boat so they can resell her, but I haven't seen anyone else climbing all over this one. We'll grab her for nearly nothing and if not, *c'est la vie.*"

"But Hanns, won't you wind up on a government list, yourself?"

"Possibly, but I'm a documented non-smuggler; that's a long story.[15] Also, our cargo will be entirely legit. If they want to waste their time searching me or following me, let them."

Two sparse cabins at the nameless freighter's deck level supported a low-ceilinged galley and dining area on top of which squatted a pilothouse – little more than a bare metal room with windows. A few modern navigation instruments and a VHF radio remained aboard, left by previous owners. Hanns turned the wheel and tried the gear and throttle linkages. "We found an ugly duckling!"

Hanns descended the stairs to the deck and hailed a uniformed man on the dock. "Do you know anything about this boat?"

"Si, Señor. I take care o' her this pas' year. She not a look so good, but I star-ta-de-engine a few weeks ago. She leak; you gotta keep de pump runnin', but she a good little freighter. I put in de 'lectric pump so you no gotta run de diesel pump alla de time. Nobody wan' her; she been here long time. You bid eight-thousan' dollars, you take her. Eight-thousan' dollars."

The rusted freighter was the last boat on a list of a few dozen being auctioned off. By the time she came up for bid, the only people left in front of the auctioneer were Werner, Hanns, Raquel, and a group of Haitian men. Werner bought the freighter 'as-is, where-is' for $7500.

"Two or three months and she's yours," Hanns explained to the disappointed Haitian bidders. "We won't need her after that and she'll be in much better shape when I'm done with her." One of the men scribbled his contact information on the back of his copy of the auction list. Hanns put the note in his pocket.

Hanns handed Raquel a pen. "This one's going in your name."

"Oh, darling. A present? For me? Really, you shouldn't have."

"The politics will go easier if you, a U.S. citizen, buy the boat from the U.S. Government. It'll be a fustercluck to put her under a German flag and then deal with bringing a foreign boat into a U.S. port. You're the owner. You're the Captain. You have an American address, right?"

"Technically, yes, but Michelle put all my stuff in storage. The landlord's an old friend; he'll pass my mail to Michelle but God only knows who's living in my old apartment."

"So much the better – another layer of anonymity and insulation."

"But why do we need that? We're not doing anything illegal."

"Sweetie, anything that separates me from government agencies, lawyers, tax collectors, salesmen, and other institutionalized scam artists will only add a measure of simplicity and tranquility as I pursue my peaceful business strategies in the land of the open palm."

Raquel rolled her eyes before leaving to get a second taxi-load of food and supplies. Hanns changed the filters, cleaned out the water separator and bled the fuel system. Two new marine batteries revealed most of the running lights to be in working order, and he installed two 12-volt marine lights in the engine room. He repacked the stuffing box where the propeller shaft exited the hull, which didn't stop the water from entering altogether but slowed the leakage.

Werner explored the ship, poking through lockers and opening hatches. He was more than a little disappointed but did his best not to show it.

An hour later, a clattering of feet reverberated on the steel deck. Hanns ascended the rusty steps. Raquel turned the light on in the galley. A half-dozen cockroaches scattered. "Y'know, Hanns, this isn't exactly luxury cruising. You drag a woman into something like this, you're gonna have to pay."

Hanns laughed. "Don't look a gift horse in the mouth. We stole this baby. Also, you know I'm all for neat and clean myself. A day or two of cleaning and painting will make her much more pleasant to run, if not more buoyant. Did you get the bug bombs?"

"A dozen of them."

"We'll fumigate the cargo hold and the cabins on the way back. Once we're home on *Chaos* in Dominica, we'll bomb the rest of her. Every room on this ship has a watertight door. The people who built this tub probably built ships for the U.S. Navy during World War II. The idea was to keep leaks, damage, or fire as isolated from the rest of the ship as possible. Steel doors work for sealing up bugs and rats with the poison, too."

"Rats?"

"Well, I haven't seen any ... but forget I said anything. Can I show you something cool?"

"As long as it's not rats, sure."

"Follow me down to the engine room."

With a large lever, Hanns turned the flywheel over slowly a few times to distribute oil through the single cylinder. Then, he gave the arm a strong pull and closed the compression lever on top of the cylinder head. A small explosion was heard and the flywheel began to slowly rotate.

Werner appeared in the engine room doorway. "Is that all? I thought..."

Boom. The flywheel turned slightly faster now.

Boom boom.

"Oh, I..."

Boom boom boom.

Boom boom boom boom.

Hanns motioned for Raquel and Werner to follow him away from the din and closed the door behind them.

"This engine has a super-heavy flywheel. It takes a short while to get going but once that weight is spinning, nothing can stop it. The sound of a single cylinder diesel starting up is delightful. You can run these machines for months at a time; they're the hardiest things on the planet."

"Spoken like a true man," observed Raquel.

"Maybe, but the engine is the saving grace of the whole ship. She has a smaller sister diesel for the main pump, too."

"Does it run?"

"Probably, but if not, we can use the electric one. They're going to start charging us dockage as of tomorrow morning so if the diesel pump won't start, we'll fix it under weigh or when we get back to Dominica."

Hanns flipped on the running lights. Raquel and Werner uncleated the dock lines and followed them aboard before joining Hanns in the pilothouse.

Raquel put a folder full of ship's papers down on the chart table." So what are we going to call her?"

"I got the idea from you, Raquel. What do you think of *Gift Horse*?"

She put an arm around Hann's waist and giggled. "More like Gift *Hearse*!"

Hanns bowed to his crew theatrically. "Four hundred miles to Dominica; we'll be home in two or three days."

"My fingers are crossed," said Werner with lighthearted cynicism. "You're sure the life raft has fewer holes than the ship?"

The dark freighter slipped around the jetty and rattled into the Puerto Rican night.

– *Currents,* 2012

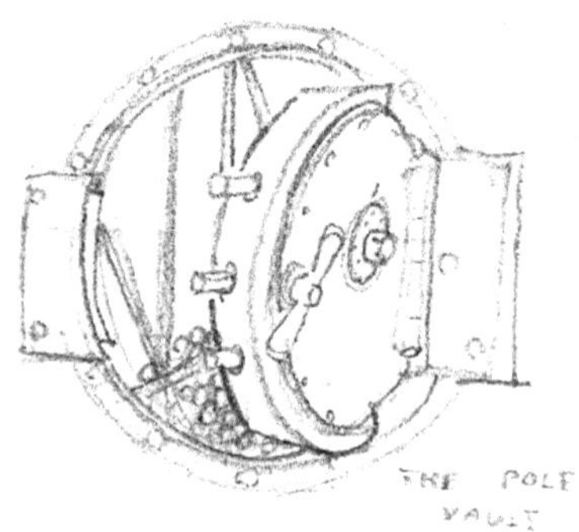

High school sketch, circa 1980

This is What We Do

SEPTEMBER – late in the season: Though tempted to linger in the enchanting Azores, we must finish our crossing to Europe. Our passage, projected to take ten or eleven days, will be easy compared to the first twenty-six-day leg of our voyage. After a summer spent in the company of yachtsmen who made passages of at least a thousand miles to share our dock, this journey is not preceded by the nervous excitement that attended its beginning.

We are sailors. This is what we do.

Each of us understands that reaching the far shore represents the terminus of a grand adventure and a transition into a less predictable realm. On the ocean, all men are equal. The sea recognizes no social classes, economic divisions, hard bosses, landowners, or toll collectors. The Atlantic may test us or terrify us or even take our lives, but to its depths we ascribe no dark motive or intent to beguile. In the realm of Poseidon, teamwork, perseverance, and clarity are coin; here, we have sufficient accounts to make our journey. Ashore, cash and influence are currency. Soon, we must rebuild our resources where men trade in different measures of labor and value.

We're broke, and Gerhard's original offer to pay me as crew (and thus the promised fare for my return trip and the rent for *Blue Monk's* mooring in the Bahamas) trades on future earnings. After adjusting to life at sea and enjoying an unanticipated vacation in the Azores, rejoining the civilized world will be our challenge.

Open water.

The wind increases.

The seas grow rough. We run downwind in huge rolling swells.

I vomit.

Matina vomits.

Gerhard vomits.

The autopilot dies.

For the next nine days, we hand-steer around the clock, seasick or not.

How big are these swells? Twenty feet? Thirty feet? More? We ride over the crests, roll over the troughs, and surf into deep valleys of black water under a colorless sky. The cockpit floods and drains. Rivers run up and down the deck, streaming out the scuppers as seas and spray climb aboard. *Journeyman* buries her bow, shudders, and rises from waves that try to swallow her.

With the VHF radio, we hail friends from São Miguel who left in a much smaller boat than ours. We can't see them but they're within range and they answer. Like us, they're uncomfortable and wet, but bashing their way eastward. Chitchatting under these circumstances is absurd, but we find futile comfort in knowing we're not alone out here.

Through the steering wheel in my hands, I sense enormous pressure against the rudder as it resists the seas trying to roll *Journeyman* on her beam-ends.[16] Nine rotations of the wheel are required to turn from one side of the steering range to the other, but even with this tremendous mechanical advantage, keeping our course requires strength and concentration. I understand why the autopilot gave up.

Standing in knee-deep water, I steer until the queasiness comes on, heave, and then recover sufficiently to continue steering again. I recall hearing of a seasickness remedy that employs elastic wristbands to push plastic beads against pressure points on the wrists. The next marine store lies nine hundred miles ahead so I improvise with duct tape and two pinto beans. Forty-five minutes later, I am singing in the cockpit, eating and drinking to keep my energy and enthusiasm up, and enjoying the scenery.

By sunset, we are wet, cold, and tired. We heave our vessel to, effectively parking for the night. With an assist from the engine, we round up into the wind, haul up the mizzen sail, and tack back across the gale without bringing the jib to the other side. The mizzen keeps *Journeyman* headed up while the backwinded jib tries to push the bow off the wind. The sails balance; we drift in relative comfort. Down below, all is soaked and in disarray but we're too exhausted to care. I sleep in my wet foul weather gear on a pile of soggy sail bags shifted onto my bunk. Hundreds of miles from land, we have plenty of sea room; we can drift without worrying about shoals and shores.

Morning light awakens me. My first thought is surprise over having slept at all. *Maybe the storm has blown out?* It feels surprisingly calm from inside the cabin. My joints ache from the dampness. I open the companionway doors and creakily ascend the steps to the cockpit.

Hove to, *Journeyman* rides comfortably among enormous swells, but contrary to first impressions, the wind has *increased.* From horizon to horizon, the surface of the ocean is a field of churning white foam. The tops of giant rollers are blasted into flying spray by the wind. I am adrift at the center of an exploding world.

Why am I not afraid?

There is no point in being afraid. There is nobody to ask for help, nobody to pay, nobody to seek advice from, no dream to wake from, no port to run to.

Three mice cling to a leaf in a tempest; what good would it do to be afraid? Nature prepares us to flee or fight but we are programmed as much to master our destinies and face our fates with cold reserve and hard resolve. There is nowhere to run, no foe to fight. We have done all we can do to ensure our safety. Survival means keeping our heads, minding the wind and seas, and pressing on.

Alone in the cockpit, I sit on the helmsman's seat watching the shattered face of the North Atlantic.

No, I am not afraid. I am blessed to bear witness to nature's secret rage on this remote part of Planet Earth. Scenes like this don't exist on the terrestrial plane.

A calm slick lingers on the water in the lee of our hull in the path of our slow drift. I see fish schooling around our keel. Perhaps *they're* seeking shelter behind *us?* I manage a smile at the irony.

I call our friends on the radio.

No answer.

I assume they're out of range.

I *hope* they're out of range.

A chainplate parts on the mizzenmast. The spar[17] rattles and vibrates, trying to jump out of its step. The restorative comfort of heaving to and the necessary hiatus it delivers from manning the wheel in boiling seas will not be possible if we lose the mizzenmast. I start the engine, which wakes Gerhard, then manage the helm while he wrestles down the sail. Up and over the swells we go and down into the troughs again.

But the gale blows from behind us.

Gibraltar lies ahead.

We are wet and tired, hungry and uncomfortable, but the wind favors our course and Gerhard has built a sturdy ship.

The day wears on.

The storm blows out, fading slowly, almost unnoticeably, spending its power like the mainspring of a great clock until it is time to haul aloft the big gaff mainsail and bend a jib to the forestay.

A pot of stew bubbles on the stove. The decks dry in the sun. Wet sail bags and sea-soaked clothing air out on the cabin top.

The storm is past.

Little is spoken of it.

We survived.

Many miles of ocean lie before us.

We adopt a new rhythm. I retire after dinner at eight o'clock while Gerhard stands watch until midnight, at which time I ascend to the cockpit with my tape player and a selection of cassettes to sing to me through the night.[18] Every night, I stare at the compass, listen to my cassettes one side at a time, and sail into a starry void. *Journeyman's* bowsprit points not across night-shrouded waves, but out into an endless beyond.

We are not floating.

We are flying through space.

I choose a star to keep in a certain place in the rigging. Every so often, I change stars or change my reference point, allowing my guiding light to shift relative to where it hovers over the mast spreader or the lightbox mounted on the shrouds. After a few nights, I learn to slowly compensate for the gradual spin of my guide stars around Polaris so they don't pull me off course. How the Polynesians navigated for thousands of miles is no great mystery. They grew up sailing under the stars, developed a sense of heaven's rhythm, and turned slowly, steadily one way as the celestial dome turned the other; they knew intuitively what stars were over what destinations at what times. I check my course against the compass less frequently, steering more and more accurately as the nights go by. The helm demands less concentration. Alone in the cockpit under the Milky Way, I experiment with controlling the speed of time, extending my four-hour watches by two or three hours to allow Gerhard more sleep. As the constellations glide across the celestial dome in a single endless moment, what is another hour or two or three? What is an hour at all?

When I am too tired to keep a straight course any longer and I've listened to my box of tapes and dawn streaks the sky before me, I wake Gerhard and give him the helm. Grateful for the extra sleep, he thanks me before I climb forward into my bunk.

During the days, we keep short, informal watches. Matina practices keeping a straight compass course as we plot tiny eastward-moving crosses on our chart.

The sun marches over our heads through a field of blue, burns the horizon beyond our wake, yields to the stars, purples the east, and rises before us again.

We are aground in a river of time.

We eat.

We sleep.

With the wheel, we turn the ocean round our boat.

Days pass like silken threads on hidden currents of wind.

Hours hover like dust revealed by a sunbeam.

Forever collapses into a moment.

Infinity reduces to zero.

There can be no other side, no destination.

There is only here, only now.

The wind falls light again.

We motor over calm, shimmering seas.

Two fishing vessels appear before us, rising slowly, steadily above the edge of the mirrored plane of the sea. We wave at the men working the boats and steer around the floats that mark the perimeters of their nets.

Gibraltar is close.

Time returns with proximity, with the notion of here and there and distance between.

No electric excitement, no air of celebration arises with the prospect of completing our Atlantic crossing. In truth, we share a subtle melancholy as more boats and birds and signs of land appear.

Suppressing thoughts of the terrestrial unknowns that lie ahead, we mind the compass, adjust the wheel, trim the sails, mark the chart, check that the bilges are dry, make a pot of coffee, stand our watches, study the waves, discuss what weather the clouds portend, and listen to the sound of the ocean moving past our hull, reveling in our journey's final endless moments of timelessness before land's inevitable arrival.

We are sailors. This is what we do.

– *The Blue Monk,* 2016

High school sketch, circa 1980

Enlightenment Enshmightenment

2017

Put a sunbeam in a jar
It disappears

Call it by name
It is separate from you

Let it warm body and spirit
It is what it is

A young yoga instructor offered a workshop in "yoga philosophy" where, as expected, she talked about Zen.

"Desire – attachment – is the root of all suffering."

Death of the Guitar

And then
At the end of her lecture
With some frustration in her voice
She said it:

"What I really want is to become enlightened."

I smiled at her beautiful, unintended lesson
What had she just been talking about?
Detaching
Letting go of desire

Try to fall asleep
You can't sleep until until you stop trying
Abandon the desire to attain enlightenment
Where are you?
What must you already be?

Enlightenment
Or happiness

Or beauty
Or peace
Is not a state you attain

It is not a degree or a badge or a hat that you wear

It is something you *are*
Not something you see yourself as being
Or not being

It is *you*
Not your identity

It is something you convey without intention
Not something you think or say you *are*

Point at it
It's gone

Am I enlightened?

Death of the Guitar

I don’t know

I don’t care

The question is not the path

Enlightenment enshmightenment

The Sailor

WHETHER FOR AN AFTERNOON OR A DECADE, for a jaunt across the lake or to make an ocean passage, it is the object of the sailor to disengage from those scripts he might otherwise write actively or passively to govern the course of his life. The sailor embarks on his journey with a compass and a watch not to submit to some predetermined overriding plan, but rather, to experience what some larger and more indeterminate collaboration between happenstance and fate holds in store for him. Each day brings a new plot, a new cast of characters, a new set of challenges or, perhaps, one of the most poignant of human callings: a challenge to resist the enticements of sirens who sing of treasures hidden among reefs and shoals, to humbly stand his watch under the stars, riding a fair wind with the deck purring beneath his feet and his tiller in hand, ready to turn the very earth at his whim.

Just as a sailing vessel travels in two worlds balanced on that thinnest of edges between ocean and sky, the mariner is a creature of *terra firma* who ventures across an aqueous landscape beneath which he cannot survive but for the briefest of intervals. He must learn to hear the subtlest of clues whispered by waves and clouds, trust his compass and above all, place his faith at times in convictions based on not the slightest of empirical foundations. The discovery of faith in self is an ages-old theme; its traditional protagonist faces his stormy seas and ultimately casts his anchor at the far shore having proven himself through his journey – or perhaps, poetically, he may be driven back by winds and seas only to discover to his surprise that he has bettered himself by attempting his journey at all.

Certainly, this accessible formula offers the comfortable clarity of a series of symbolic obstacles and some manner of redemption that qualifies the turning of a book's final leaf, but the terminus of our own life's adventure is rarely so characterized by goals accomplished, debts paid, oceans traversed, and dragons slain. Life is but a series of journeys undertaken, and in the case of the mariner, most often by men and women who have cultivated sufficient mettle to warrant exclusion from that classic writer's formula.

Beyond his struggle to survive as an animal in a natural world, the sailor must survive as a man in a world of men. He has a vessel to maintain and must develop the requisite skills and acquire the necessary funds to keep his course.

For the financial elite, the option to hire captains, navigators, and laborers to bend sails and scrape barnacles from the keel presents itself, and perhaps then, there is room for elements of the classic stories after all? There is that oft-written parable of the king who cannot exchange his gold for his predicament and must depend on the good character of the peasant hero, but real life looms larger than that. The purpose of the true cruising sailor is to simply and unpretentiously *go sailing*, possibly without any specific destination in mind, any significant quantity of cash on-hand, or any great personal challenge to meet.

The mariner navigates his craft, offers his services as a laborer when he can, and day by day, mile by mile, he accumulates a journal of experiences and a scattered network of co-conspirators who collectively form the tapestry of a life lived richly, deeply, and unusually. His sole redemption for wresting his hull from the grip of a reef may be the humble gift of survival to limp, broken, into the next port, yet, given the character of his quest, the chance to make such a colorful entry in his logbook is a grand opportunity.

The mariner must occasionally tie his painter[19] to the shore and navigate the corals and currents of civilization. When he returns to his tiller, if he is true to his purpose, he returns to confront challenges that, though severe at times, are unburdened by human folly. A reef or a stormy sea may destroy his vessel and take his life, yet such hazards are not acts of sapient malice or sabotage.

There is some comfort in this, but where there is wind, there are waves and where there is land, there are dangerous shallows. It is, ironically, in the lee of a protecting shore where the sailor finds shelter from turbulent seas. Even in the middle of great oceans, he is a creature bound ultimately to the soil from whence he came. When he voyages forth upon the swells, he carries his humanity with him in all of its greatness and contradiction, and in tropical paradises, in congress with his fellows, his struggle remains ultimately to pursue the grandest and oldest of all classic themes – the search for meaning.

With good characters and colorful places left so often behind in the wake of his story's progress, the reader may wonder where, on this stage where tranquil anchorages, ocean swells, and hazardous reefs mix with scattered expressions of humanity, is this all going? What is the great challenge? What is the final reward? But life is rarely so neatly packaged. The story of our protagonist's journey is like our own – a series of successive storms, calms, crossings, and harbors that under the best of circumstances, culminates humbly with preparations for another voyage. The reader is advised therefore not to anticipate a final step from deck to dock, but rather, to keep a weather eye out and mind the wind he races before. Like the best of sailing voyages, the importance of the destination is far secondary to figuring out, by wit or by wisdom, exactly where in the world one happens to be at any given moment.

But lo, the glass rises.

The gale freshens.

Poseidon favors our passage.

Aweigh.

Aweigh.

– *Waves,* 2011

High school sketch, circa 1980

The Sea Cucumber

1981

Across the bottom of the ocean
Does the sea cucumber plod
A big long green example
Of the phylum Gastropod

I know this to be true
(It says so right here in my notes)
If you disturb the sea cucumber
It will blow its oats

It barfs its bodily organs out
With a mighty cucumber heave
In hopes that any predator
Its entrails will deceive

Death of the Guitar

It blows its insides out
And though a predator may chew
It won't be upon the sea cucumber
It'll just have a mouth full of spew

The clever sea cucumber then
Crawls back into its den
Its insides gone, it waits
Until it grows them back again

And though, my friend, you might feel
That this story's made you sick
You must admit the sea cucumber's
Got a pretty fancy trick

Now, think about it
Don't you ever wish you, too, were able
To vomit all your organs out
Upon the dining table?

Why everyone around you
Would put up such a fuss!
I guess the sea cucumber's just
A step ahead of us

High school sketch, circa 1980

Nighteagle on the Reef

NIGHTEAGLE RAN SWIFTLY BEFORE THE GALE. A John Alden schooner built in the 1920s and a survivor of military service as a U-boat patrol craft during World War II, her sleek black hull sliced through the seas. On watch was her owner, Luis, a large Italian man with a stern jaw and a scar on his cheek. Below slept his hired crew, secure against the lee cloths that kept them in their bunks.

Luis inhaled deeply from his cigarette and let the smoke stream from his nostrils. He locked the wheel brake, steadied himself against the end of the heavy spruce main boom and urinated over the side.

It was nearly dawn. Mayaguana was at least sparsely populated with an airstrip and some shelter. There was a reef off Pirate Well settlement, but behind it were shoals and a soft, sandy beach. This would be as good a time and place as any. Luis checked the lashings on the dinghy to make sure they could be released easily.

Bennet and Mimi snuggled together like spoons in the starboard bunk in the main saloon. Red slept in the port bunk. *It's good nobody is sleeping up forward,* thought Luis for a moment. He raised his eyebrows, becoming uncomfortably aware he didn't much care one way or the other.

A few lights flickered on shore but no contours of land could be seen behind the mountainous Atlantic swells.

Luis zipped up his sea jacket, put on a life vest and aimed for the lights. The trick would be to approach at an angle.

Before he was really quite ready, *Nighteagle* was in the breakers. "Reef! Reef! All hands! All hands on deck!"

He spun the wheel to port and the *Nighteagle* glanced twice off the reef before settling on top of a coral head.

Red, a short, sturdy man with a cinnamon beard and a blotchy tan made of coagulated freckles, was first on deck. He helped Mimi up through the companionway, taking her hand. The vessel heeled and rocked as waves broke over her from abeam.

Bennet turned on the cabin light. Calm under pressure; his deep set oceanic blue eyes glowed under a pair of movie star eyebrows and a salty mop of sandy hair. "We're taking on water up forward. We're holed! Let's get some fenders and cushions between the boat and these rocks."

Another big wave exploded over the deck. The hull made crunching sounds as it rocked on top of the coral with the advance and retreat of the waves.

Bennet dutifully drew a large inflatable docking fender from a cockpit locker and dropped it between the spastic, lurching hull and the coral. The next big wave brought *Nighteagle* down hard on it, exploding it like a grenade.

Luis grabbed the main mast with one hand and the shrouds with the other. "Abandon ship. Let's get this dinghy in the water before she breaks up."

Bennet came up from the cabin and helped ready the dinghy for launch. Mimi tied her Scandinavian blonde hair up in a ponytail and gathered some photographs and personal effects into a rubberized duffel bag along with a few bottles of water and some fruit. In five minutes, the inflatable was launched and sitting in the relatively sheltered area between the grounded hull of the *Nighteagle* and the coral.

Red spoke up. "I see dawn on the horizon. We're way up on these rocks and the tide is going out. We ain't gonna sink any time soon. Let's wait till we can see what the damage is."

Luis was ready to get off the boat, but the crashing breakers were scarier than he'd imagined and it made sense to leave when they could see their way up and around the dangerous coral, especially in a vulnerable inflatable dinghy.

An hour later, the sky turned purple and *Nighteagle* lay heeled atop a large coral head with thirty feet of water on her port side and barely a foot on the other.

Luis coughed and spit over the side. "Let's go. I want out of here. She's finished."

Red grabbed his bag out of the dinghy and threw it down the companionway onto the starboard bunk. "I ain't a goin'. Y'all can do what you want, but this boat ain't sinkin' long as she's up on this coral, and there ain't no reason we can't patch her up and git her sailin' again.

"Whaddya think, Ben?"

Mimi was scared, but looked into her boyfriend's eyes.

Bennet looked at Luis. "C'mon … Red's right. We can rig some sort of a patch job, pump her out and get her floating. Let's give her a try. The tide's still going down and we have almost ten hours before the water comes back up."

Luis looked down. "Abandon ship! I don't want anyone getting hurt, We're out here on a reef in a goddamned gale. This is no place for heroics. It's just a boat. Everyone … in the dinghy … now!"

Red stood on the deck. "I ain't a goin'."

"I gave an order."

"Abandon this boat and I'll be the one giving orders."

"This is mutiny!"

"No sir, this is insurance fraud. We either patch this boat and move on, or *you* abandon ship and I have as much right to try to salvage her as some stranger on Mayaguana. Anyone with me?"

Bennet grabbed Mimi's hand and they climbed out of the dinghy. "Sorry, Luis. Nothing personal but I'm with Red on this one. If you want to abandon ship, you can head out and according to the chart, you'll see where the breakers end a few hundred yards northwest of us. But all the damage will be above the water level when the tide goes out, and with a little luck, we can float her on the next high tide. I don't see what you have to lose by trying, but if you want to go, I'm afraid I just have to wish you luck."

"If I ever see you guys again, you'd better believe there'll be a warrant out for the thieves who stole my boat. This is mutiny and…"

"Save it," Red said calmly. "You can't abandon a boat and then get your dress up over your head when someone else salvages it. Either stay and help or shut the fuck up and get out of here. Don't forget to write."

Luis said nothing. Clenching his jaw, he started the outboard and motioned for Bennet to untie the bow and stern lines from the dinghy. The new owners of the *Nighteagle* watched the dinghy motor slowly north and then, apparently having passed the reef line, Luis headed for the white, sandy shore.

"Asshole." Red stood on the canted deck.

"Maybe, but we're thirty-one different flavors of committed at this point. What's your plan?"

"First off, there's some planks and tarpaulins down in the cockpit lockers We're going to need some sort of work surface; that coral is no place to be sitting or standing. There's some lead pigs in the bilge and a rusted out old anchor that should be the first official piece of jetsam from our new schooner. Let's put some boots on, get them planks put out by the bow, and weigh them down with the anchor and some lead so we have somethin' to walk on.

"Then, I wanna get that hard dinghy off the cabin top. We're gonna have to get some anchors hauled out and set off to windward.'

"Mimi, can you get up inside the bow with a screwdriver and a pry bar where the damage is? There's a teak ceiling[20] up there that ain't doin' nothin' but standing between us and the hull. If it's already broken, bust the boards out with the pry bar. If we can save any of it, unscrew it and stash it somewhere. Just holler if you need some muscle."

"Nope. I got it." Mimi managed a smile. The boat had stopped rocking by now and the whole day was turning into an unexpected adventure on a strange, submerged island. If at the end of the day, they didn't have their own fifty-two-foot schooner, they'd at least have a dinghy to row ashore in and a good story to tell.

Bennet helped get planks put down and propped up where the coral beneath them was off-level. Red stood next to the hull with water alternatively swirling around his knees and flooding out. Bennet looked from above over the starboard bulwark as Red inspected the damage. "We got us a two-foot jagged hole 'bout a foot under the water line. There's some wooden boat tools in the locker under the chart table. Do you know how to make a big fat chisel good 'n' sharp?"

"Sure do." Bennet retrieved the tool. It was still dry in the main cabin, and the tools were unaffected by the water that had entered the boat. The bilge pumps had drained all of it except for a foot-deep pool forward where the angle of the boat kept the water from flowing where they could get to it. Bennet oiled up a whetstone, put a fine double-bevel on the end of the chisel and brought it forward to Red along with a good-sized mallet.

Hammer blows reverberated against the wood of *Nighteagle*'s hull as Red chopped away splintered planks and fragments; anything that wasn't structurally sound. Satisfied, he handed the tools back up to Bennet.

"How's the water level?"

"Ain't changed much; must be slack low tide. We gotta get movin' if we're gonna catch this train.

"Good news is there ain't much compound curve to the hull in this section. It's pretty much flat. Can you hand me the tape measure?"

Red disappeared under the hull with it for a moment and then came back up. Can you cut me two pieces of that plywood 'bout three-foot by two-foot-six? There should be some pieces in there jus' wide enough. If the generator ain't wet, you can use the jigsaw in the port cockpit locker."

Bennet found a scrap piece already cut to size, and used it as a pattern for the second.

"Ben, take one of them pieces up forward and push it hard against the hole from inside. Get me a pencil and I'm gonna trace the outline of the hole on the wood from the outside."

After a slip or two, the outline was drawn. Bennet used the electric saw to cut around the outline of the hole and then used that piece as a pattern for two more per Red's instructions.

"Now make me up a 'layer cake' with the full piece on the inside of the hull and the hole-shaped pieces screwed and caulked together on top. Use the electric drill as a screw gun; see if you can scrounge up some bronze wood screws.

"Mimi, you know how to mix epoxy?"

"I've done it a time or two."

"Good. We'll need two batches. The first one needs lots of filler. Make it thick like peanut butter. We need to kick it off fast 'cause we don't have much time, but if you kick it off too hard, it'll boil. If you mix the epoxy and the filler, I'll climb up and add the hardener myself. For the second batch, we want to keep it thin. I found some fiberglass cloth in the lazarette. If we can get the epoxy to kick off before the water comes up, we'll have ourselves an ugly-but-strong repair job."

Bennet worked with the drill and assembled the patch, showing it proudly to Red.

"Get up there with the drill and the extension cord and screw that thing into the good wood around the hole. Put a shitload of caulking in there where the overlap is, too."

As Bennet worked from the inside, Red mixed hardener into the thickened epoxy and troweled it into the voids between the patch and the hull and then over the top in as good an approximation as he could make of the hull's original curve. Following up with two layers of fiberglass cloth, he saturated the area with fast-drying epoxy, finishing about the same time Red finished screwing the patch to the hull from the inside.

As expected, the water came up by afternoon, but the patch held.

"Hand me a line, and let's haul that rusty-ass anchor back up. I got one more use for it, after all." Red attached the line and helped Bennet lift it back over the bulwark into the lee scupper before clambering back aboard.

The *Nighteagle* began to rock as the water lifted her, but the winds and seas had moderated; the crunching sounds were less violent.

Red and Bennet lifted the wooden dinghy from where it was lashed, inverted it on the cabin top, and wrestled the heavy craft over the side.

"There's some rusty-ass chain to go with that rusty-ass anchor and some funky old line. Let's get a hook set as far out as we can find bottom that ain't a million miles deep, and get ready to crank this sucker off when the tide comes up. Once we're free, we'll dump the anchor and sail on."

Red rowed out into the swells as far as the line would allow and dropped the hook. "Pull in on that line and make sure she's holding."

Bennet hauled in twenty or thirty feet of rode and signaled a thumbs up. "She's set!"

Red returned and they muscled the dinghy back on-deck.

"Sure we won't need it in the water?" asked Mimi.

"Think positive. We're going sailing, and don't need to be bailin' out no dinghies out in the big ocean."

Red attached a turning block[21] to the end of the main halyard and then snapped the block onto the anchor line. Bennet smiled and Mimi looked at him quizzically.

"Go ahead … Ask, Mimi … You wanna know why I'm attaching the anchor to the top of the mast?"

"The question did occur to me; yes."

"Mechanical advantage. We're gonna have a small window of highest-high tide to get this sucker rolled over the other way and dragged off. We're either gonna crank this boat off this reef or break this mast tryin'. If we can bust her loose, we'll push her the rest of the way off with the engine and then we're all goin' cruisin'."

The sun dropped lower in the sky. *Nighteagle* came almost upright and began to bounce on the coral again.

Red stood on the deck with crossed arms. "It's 'bout time. Let's fire up the engine and get out of here. Bennet, crank in on that anchor windlass nice and slow."

Bennet cranked back on the handle and the line creaked under the tension.

"Give it some more. Ain't no use holdin' back. It'll either work or it won't."

Red engaged the throttle and pushed the diesel hard.

Nighteagle bumped on the coral, bounced upright, and slowly spun her bow seaward.

"Keep crankin'. Pull that sucker. We're movin'!"

A swell rolled in, slamming the keel hard against the coral one more time. *Nighteagle* lurched forward and sailed free. Bennet freed the anchor line from the windlass, and watched it fly through the block and slip into the waiting sea.

– *Waves,* 2011

Clichés

October, 2013

SINCE TIME IMMEMORIAL, clichés have sneaked in the door when we least expect them. They're low-hanging fruit for writers who abscond with them quickly instead of striving for excellence. But to the trained eye, writing clichés stick out like a sore thumb. Authors of this day and age who struggle under the yoke of undetected style errors are too numerous to mention. The good writer puts his nose to the grindstone and embarks on a quest to find hidden treasure. With the patience of Job, he leaves no stone unturned in his search for words and phrases that give his writing a personal, authentic voice.

Writers from all walks of life are determined to publish by hook or by crook. Champing at the bit to publish his book, the writer gets behind the eight ball and pours himself lock, stock, and barrel into the task of writing. Cool as a cucumber and lost in contemplation, the ambitious author taps away at the keyboard day in and day out until the crack of dawn, happy as a kid in a candy store. As his manuscript grows by leaps and bounds, he envisions a whirlwind bookstore tour and expects his book to sell like hotcakes. Sure of success, he pulls out all the stops and pours everything but the kitchen sink into his writing. And he's proud to have sufficient skill as a writer to avoid paying through the nose for an expensive editor. Publishing, he is certain, will open the floodgates to a world of opportunity where there's never a dull moment. He envisions untold wealth, living larger than life in the lap of luxury, and laughing all the way to the bank.

But this flurry of activity is actually the calm before the storm. The pie-in-the-sky dream is too good to be true. Such writers are accidents waiting to happen. In this dog-eat-dog world, such books are usually dead in the water, and at best they're a flash in the pan. Give the devil his due; the writing is on the wall for this author. His own worst enemy, he fails to realize that his chances are one in a million. Little the wiser, he jumps the gun and publishes before you can say "Jack Robinson." At the end of the day, how many of his words fall on deaf ears? He falls hook, line, and sinker for the fantasy of becoming a bestselling author. Then, to add insult to injury, he hangs on to the bitter end, enjoying at best only a checkered career before his book is buried beneath the sands of time and forgotten by the long march of history. For all intents and purposes, in the twinkling of an eye, he's dead as a doornail.

It goes without saying that the winds of change have brought higher standards to the fast-maturing world of self-publishing. Self-publishers are all in the same boat. To tame the wild horse of the publishing world, we must all pay the piper and nip bad writing habits in the bud.

Clichés are only one problem among many that writers should avoid like the plague. Each and every one of us must take the tiger by his tail and think outside the box. New words and phrases are easy to find or create for those willing to take the journey. The challenge to find clever words is hardly a search for a needle in a haystack. Why use clichés over and over when there are plenty of fish in the sea? Why live the writer's life on borrowed time? After all, you can't make a silk purse out of a sow's ear. Make no bones about it; writers who count their chickens before they're hatched will soon find them coming home to roost. The ball's in your court. Take the bull by the horns, bite the bullet, go back to the drawing board, and add some clever new phrases to your bag of writing tricks. Open up that can of worms in your writing before you publish and share them. The acid test for good writing is authenticity. Well-constructed prose is a breath of fresh air, not a rehash of the same old same old. Learn the ropes. Dot your i's and cross your t's. Knuckle down and honor the craft of writing.

All things considered, it's probably a fool's errand to try to rid your writing of clichés entirely, but in a nutshell, it stands to reason that in the cold light of day, weak writing habits will all come out in the wash. Publishing without paying your dues is like banging your head against a brick wall. Instead of shooting yourself in the foot, take the high road. The path to excellence is as plain as the nose on your face. Play your cards right, face the music, strike while the iron's hot, and turn over a new leaf.

You'll find no hard and fast rules about what's cliché and what's not, but by the same token, writers who exercise discerning judgment about their wordcraft are head and shoulders above the rest. Practice makes perfect. Put your best foot forward and work slowly but surely until your writing becomes as steady as a rock. For all intents and purposes, your prose need not meet the lofty standards of the average ivory tower stick in the mud, but when it comes down to the nitty-gritty, polished writing is a rare beast indeed and not anything to be sneezed at.

Without a shadow of a doubt, too many authors make the same mistakes *ad infinitum.* Gluttons for punishment, they dismiss previous, failed efforts as water under the bridge and part of the learning curve, then forge ahead. Come hell or high water, they're determined to earn the glowing tributes, thunderous applause, and choruses of approval that only a chosen few are blessed to receive once in a blue moon.

But there's no such thing as a free lunch. Publishing is a game of survival of the fittest. Ignorance is bliss. Mark my words, the time has come to stop muddying the waters of short, sweet, and to the point writing with the cast-off jetsam and flotsam of language. The unvarnished truth: writers who fail to heed this warning will get their just desserts. Proof of the pudding is that left high and dry, and subject to twenty-twenty hindsight, they cry "sour grapes" at the moment of truth, and tuck their tails between their legs. With ruffled feathers, they throw in the towel and meet the untimely end of their literary lives.

As luck would have it, capable writers are not expected to be able to quote the thesaurus chapter and verse. Becoming a capable writer does not involve reinventing the wheel. As a matter of fact, there's no need to make a mountain out of a mole hill; becoming cliché-aware requires no painstaking investigation. There's no need to search your writing high and low – and ultimately, whether a phrase is "officially" cliché or not is anybody's guess. Cultivating an ability to recognize clichés is nothing to write home about. Not to put too fine a point on it, writers who seek out and expose themselves to one of the many online lists of clichés will, after due consideration, naturally incorporate their new-found awareness into their writing.

First and foremost, those writers who ultimately hit the nail on the head are the ones who recognize that battling style errors is part of the long haul every one of us must make. The completion of a rough draft is a mixed blessing. The savvy author must put his money where his mouth is, stick to the straight and narrow, pay his dues, and turn his diamond in the rough into a polished gem. Writers worth their salt know that the first draft is only the tip of the iceberg.

Great writing requires tender loving care and when the work is done, the polished writer may yet wind up an unsung hero. Excellent writing won't necessarily make or break a book and regrettably, some authors grow sick and tired enough to give up, get some well-earned rest, and publish, warts and all. But make no mistake, you get what you pay for. Your excellent book may not make you rich but you can bet your bottom dollar it will be a sight for sore eyes in a world where quality and attention to detail are sorely needed. If you don't care, who will?

Last but not least, just for the record, this essay is hardly short and sweet but there's a tongue-in-cheek method to my madness. As strange as it may seem, I sincerely hope that readers who take my words with a grain of salt will see them as a blessing in disguise.

Saturnalia

JOHN NATION AND I sit on the deck of *Zebra Dun* in Man-O-War Harbour. Diana rows over to visit. She and Richard have had a little too much togetherness over on *Killer Tomato;* thirty-two feet isn't much space to share sometimes, especially when you're not doing much sailing. Man-O-War Cay is a perfect place to just sit and be, but one can only tolerate so much sitting and so much being before one has to go sit and be somewhere else with someone else.

Diana complains for a few minutes. In her late forties, she's looking for a relationship that's more serious than being Richard's boating accessory, but having escaped her fiberglass confines, she soon decompresses and reverts to her usual, bubbly self.

Diana points to *Rabbit*, a white sloop with an unusual, rounded stern anchored nearby. "Have you met Doc?" she asks.

We shake our heads.

The boat's been here as long as we have, stored on a mooring in the protected lagoon. We don't even notice *Rabbit* anymore, which is why we both missed that, today, someone is aboard; a dinghy is tied behind her.

"I used to work with Doc back in Palm Beach when I was a nurse," Diana explains. "He's a physician. He bought the boat to retire on but he hasn't gotten to use it much. Now, he's shut down his practice. He's here in the Abacos for a while. You'll like him; he's a really sweet guy."

On cue, Doc appears in his cockpit. Diana calls to him and waves him over. Soon a short, silver-haired man with permanently hunched shoulders joins us on deck. Quiet and intelligent, Doc shows all the signs of recent arrival, like someone who went into the light not knowing what to expect and awoke in a strange world swathed in vivid blues and greens. He's still adjusting, opening his eyes – a process that takes some time; the land of clocks and calendars is not easily forsaken. "I hope…" he says slowly, "I hope I can stay here a while. I've dreamed of getting away, but my family thinks I'm crazy. 'It's not safe for someone your age,' they say. 'Surely, you must be lonely on a boat by yourself.' I worked hard for forty years and now that I can finally get what I've waited so long for, my kids and grandkids can't stop coming up with plans to 'keep the old man entertained.'"

Sitting in a folding chair on the *Zebra Dun's* mahogany deck, Doc closes his eyes and breathes deep, traveling back in time, carrying his present with him. He smiles. For now, he's here, doing what he wants to do. He's been missing a simple, intangible *something*.

Like these islands, John's wooden schooner suggests a certain other-worldliness. I have no quarrels with fiberglass boats; they have their advantages and I happen to live on one, but the unique sounds, smells, and images associated with traditional wooden boats connect one more readily to history, romance, and tradition. A handcrafted wooden vessel has stories to tell, and suggests by reference that those who sail aboard her will, too. Many yachtsmen carry a Jolly Roger ensign but few fly those colors without an air of cheap costumery. When the skull and bones are hauled to the masthead of the *Zebra Dun,* the effect is striking and authentic.

In a former life, before he got a divorce and a wooden schooner, John directed a planetarium in Oklahoma. He describes how we are about to experience a rare triple conjunction of Saturn, Uranus and Neptune. Such planetary alignments, he explains, have been blamed for wars and earthquakes, floods and famines, momentous political shifts, flashes of technological innovation, and bursts of creative expression. As we speak, astrologers sharpen pencils and put fresh ribbons in typewriters, scouring the news for important events and catastrophes to validate the profound effects of the celestial alignment. Astronomers polish mirrors and lenses in powerful telescopes. In Washington, DC, President Reagan is warned by top advisers not to make major policy decisions until the conjunction passes.

John never lost his boyhood fascination with the stars. He grows more and more animated as he holds court on deck, describing how the celestial bodies, with the exception of distant Pluto, orbit the sun in alignment, almost as a set of concentric, elliptical rings – though debate over the validity of Pluto's status as an official planet remains open. Each satellite orbits at a different speed; it's rare enough that any two are at the same point of orbit at the same time. Tomorrow night there will be three.

Once, in Marsh Harbour, while waiting to use a shower provided to cruisers by the Tiki Hut bar as an enticement to buy drinks, I happened to glance up as a rocket was climbing into the sky. We were nearly at the same latitude as Cape Canaveral, and because the U.S. doesn't launch potentially dangerous rockets over the heads of its own citizens, this one was aimed over the heads of the citizens of these northernmost islands of the Bahamas. In fact, large pieces of recovered booster rocket heat shield lean against a mahogany tree in the yard of a Man-O-War fisherman. Through the louvered door of the shower,

John heard my exclamation about the rocket. In an instant, he was standing on the dock, dripping wet, clad only in a towel, narrating the stages of the launch, oblivious to the surprised expressions of a crowd of onlookers.

Today, whether at the simple peak of his enthusiasm or affected, himself, by the growing confluence of planetary gravity, John pauses to take a breath. "We are going to have ourselves a saturnalia," he proclaims.

"How much money you got, Bricker?" he asks. A number of John's proclamations are followed by this unfortunate question.

"About four or five dollars."

"That ought to do it. I have a few dollars left and a cast-iron Dutch oven stashed under the bridge deck behind the wood stove. Between us, we can afford a chicken and some brown sugar, some vegetables, and some fresh garlic. Tomorrow, let's sail over to Shell Island where it's dark and the viewing horizon is low. We'll build a fire and roast us up a chicken to honor the pagan gods."

"Doc? Diana? Join us? Richard's welcome if you can get him to move, Diana."

"I'm in," says Doc without hesitation.

Diana nods over her shoulder at the *Killer Tomato* and rolls her eyes. "Not much chance of getting mister I-never-sail-on-the-boat-I-happen-to-be-retired-in-the-Bahamas-on to do much of anything. I'm afraid it's going to be a bachelors' night out for you guys."

After lunch the next day, *Blue Monk* follows *Zebra Dun* through the narrow, rocky cut out of Man-O-War Harbour. Doc is not far behind on *Rabbit.* We turn to starboard, heading northwest across the Little Bahama Bank. A mild norther is blowing. The wind on our beam should make for ideal sailing but we're in the lee of the out-islands much of the time; the breeze is light. We motor-sail to ensure we reach our destination with daylight to spare. Leaving Man-O-War Cay behind, we pass the low, rocky islets of the Fowl Cays Sea Park, privately-owned Scotland Cay, and the comparatively lengthy coast of Great Guana Cay, which accounts for almost half of our thirteen-mile journey.

At the end of Great Guana Cay is Whale Cay passage; a deep-water entrance from the North Atlantic Ocean to the Abaco banks. No place to be in unsettled weather, the seas in this cut pile up in ten-foot swells even when the wind is light. Local folklore says there are many boats on the bottom here. Whale Cay, itself, is a barren, rocky hump, swept clean by angry waves. Undeterred by big seas, enormous cruise ships make their way through the cut onto the banks into a sheltered, dredged mooring area. The cruise lines have developed the northwest end of Guana Cay into a private beach paradise with bars, t-shirt stands, and calypso bands – everything a sun and alcohol-seeking vacationer might desire.

But no ships are moored here today. Party beach is not our destination. Neither will we traverse Whale Cay Passage on this voyage.

Two thousand feet southwest of the ship mooring area, the dredge spoils from its creation form a small, sandy islet, unofficially dubbed "Shell Island" by cruisers. As with Pluto's bid for planethood, Shell Island has not been around long enough to be awarded official "island" status by cartographers. The unpretentious mound of sand mixed with millions of seashells and covered with scattered, scrubby grass patches, appears as little more than a shoal on our charts, but the tiny cay offers an excellent anchorage for our purpose. Shell Island provides shelter from the swells rolling through the cut, has neither trees nor high hills to obscure our view of the sky and is far from any lights that would interfere with our night vision. Apart from those we carry aboard our boats, the closest man-made lights are two miles away. Shell Island is a wild place, a speck of sand frequently passed and seldom visited. No other human presence mars this beach – no tourists, no fishermen, no Haitian refugees, no customs officials, no traffic lights or grocery stores – only three disparate planets brought together by happenstance and fate. Shell Island is primitive, secluded, and remote – the ideal place for our saturnalia.

The sun falls below the pines of Great Abaco.

The wind picks up.

The temperature drops.

We drag my dinghy to the top of the beach and prop it on its oars behind us to serve as a windbreak. John had the foresight to gather dry firewood back at Man-O-War Cay. We add to his collection a few pieces of driftwood we find on the beach. Behind our dinghy shelter, a small flame begins to consume our branches and wood scraps.

Soon, yellow sparks crackle and fly high into the fast-darkening night.

Stars gather overhead.

John points into the brilliant sky. "See the three planets grouped in a small triangle there? They're what we've come here for. They won't appear this close together again for over a thousand years."

It honestly doesn't look like much. On a moonless night in Abaco, the sky is one massive cluster of stars, anyway. But one excuse for being here is as good as another. A conjunction of planets is but the magic stone in our experiential soup, imparting mysterious flavors and mystical healing properties as surely as our own presence renders sacred this simple hill of dredge tailings at the edge of a shallow sea. Painted orange by firelight, our three spirit-faces hover before the darkness. The north wind is cold, but we are warm in the shelter of the propped-up dinghy before the flames.

The chicken, cooked with sliced carrots and onions in the iron pot over our humble fire, is delicious. Like happy savages, we strip the bones and toss them into the fire.

The celestial event brings no floods, earthquakes, or political revolutions – no grand strokes of insight, no bursts of creative inspiration. We are but three small men huddled before a flame atop a tiny mound of shells beneath the Milky Way, but the repercussions of this chance arrangement of lights in the sky are large enough for us.

Doc is quiet and reflective.

His eyes sparkle in the firelight.

It is clear this is a moment imagined and waited for since childhood, a long-awaited escape, a hoped-for connection to the deeper and simpler, a purification, an unlearning, an ascension to the mountaintop, a peeling away of layers to expose the core. "I have a heart condition," he says softly. "I'm not going to live forever. If I am to go, why not tonight beneath these stars?"

We sit together in silence as the flames die down.

The chill wind overpowers the warmth of the waning fire.

It's late.

A red moon rises above the horizon, brightens the sky, and washes away the dimmer stars.

A hundred feet off the beach, our vessels bob quietly in the loom of their anchor lights. We launch our dinghies; return to warm, waiting bunks; and sleep as one can only sleep after a day of sailing and a full plate of dinner.

In the morning, Doc pulls his anchors and heads back to his mooring at Man-O-War Cay. John and I wave and set a divergent course slightly farther south across the Sea of Abaco to Marsh Harbour on the mainland.

A week later, we return to our usual anchoring spots at Man-O-War.

Rabbit sits peacefully on her mooring but no dinghy is tied behind her.

"He had to go home for a while," Diana explains. "Family matters."

We don't see him again.

– *The Blue Monk,* 2016

Thoughts on Thanksgiving

2017

When the urge to gripe arises, consider that no matter what dark clouds may loom on the horizon, you threaded the needle of human history. Imagine what life would have been like had you been born not so many years ago. This Thanksgiving note offers a few things to think about and be thankful for. Some of them have their dark sides; the automobile and the television are as much a curse as a blessing. But for all our problems, this is the best time in human history to have ever lived. We have the best communication, the best tools, the best toys, the best travel options, the best medicine, and the best opportunities of any generation that has ever walked the planet.

I'm not unmindful of the fact that we have plenty of work to do. We have inequalities to deal with. We haven't gotten rid of war yet. Guns and politics stink. The environment is a big concern. Too many people still don't have access to luxuries we take for granted. But if you are fortunate enough to live in a developed country during this tiny slice of the 20,000-year span of human history, be thankful – even for some of the things you probably complain about. You are incredibly lucky.

Antibiotics

Have you ever prevented or cured an infection? It wasn't until the 1940s that antibiotics (Penicillin) became widely accessible to the general public.

In 1900, the three leading causes of death were pneumonia, tuberculosis (TB), and diarrhea and enteritis, which (together with diphtheria) caused one third of all deaths. Of these deaths, 40% were children aged less than 5 years. The 1918 influenza pandemic resulted in 20 million deaths, including 500,000 in the United States in less than one year – more than have died in as short a time during any war or famine in the world.

- Before antibiotics, 90% of children with bacterial meningitis died. Among those who lived, most had severe and lasting disabilities ranging from deafness to mental retardation.

- Strep throat was sometimes fatal.

- Common ear infections sometimes spread to the brain, causing severe problems.

Other common infections from tuberculosis to pneumonia to whooping cough were caused by aggressive bacteria, and led to serious illness and sometimes death.

I am grateful.

The Automobile

How old were you when you got your first car? How many miles do you drive every week? How much of your life will you spend at the wheel? At the beginning of the century the automobile entered the transportation market as a toy for the rich. The Ford Motor Company produced 1,700 cars during its first full year of business. Henry Ford produced the Model T to be an economical car for the average American. By 1920 Ford had sold over a million cars. Before that, horses, ships, and good old-fashioned walking were your best options for travel. As much as I hate traffic, what a privilege it is to fly down the highway at 70MPH! I am grateful.

Anesthesia

Have you ever had a broken bone set, a tooth drilled, a wound stitched, or a surgical procedure? Had you been born earlier, you might not have had such a painless experience. Though opium, ether, chloroform, and cocaine were used as anesthesia throughout much of human history when available, Novocain wasn't invented until 1905. The hollow hypodermic needle wasn't invented until 1898. Intravenous anesthetics were introduced in 1929. If you've ever benefited from modern anesthesia, be thankful.

Electricity and Lighting

Isn't it wonderful to walk into a dark room and flip a switch? *Click:* Instant illumination! Electricity didn't become common in American homes until the 1930s – less than a century ago. I am grateful.

Air Travel

If you fly for business, vacations, or to visit friends and family members, consider that not long ago, a steam ship would have been your only option for comfortable and safe long-distance traveling. The airplane was invented in 1903. The first commercial airline flight happened in 1914, but air travel was expensive for a long time. A ticket on TWA in 1955 from Chicago to Phoenix cost

$138 round-trip. Adjusted for inflation, that's $1,168. Air travel didn't become affordable until the late 20th century when jumbo jets became popular. I still like window seats on planes; too many generations never had the chance to look *down* on the clouds.

The Internet

If you shop, plan your schedule, research information, promote your business, sell products and services, or communicate online, consider that the World Wide Web didn't become popular and commercial until the 1990s. Amazon opened on July 5, 1994. EBay opened on Sept 3, 1995. These amazing resources are all new and recent. I am grateful.

Smartphones

What would life be like without your smartphone? Motorola became the first company to produce a handheld mobile phone on April 3, 1973. Today, millions of people are lost and out of touch without one. The first true smartphone – the Simon Personal Communicator – made its debut in 1992. It was created by IBM more than 15 years before Apple released the iPhone in 2007. The first Symbian phone, the touchscreen Ericsson R380 Smartphone, was released in 2000. It was the first device marketed as a "smartphone." My phone has a GPS, an endless array of useful apps, a web browser, email, messaging capability, etc. I am grateful.

Paved Roads

Have you ever stopped (sorry for the pun) to appreciate how wonderful it is to live in a time when you can drive on smooth, paved roads from your driveway in Key West to your friend's house in Anchorage, Alaska? America's First Transcontinental Highway, the Lincoln Highway wasn't officially dedicated until October 31, 1913. It stretched from Times Square in New York City to Lincoln Park in San Francisco. Only decades earlier, the trip required a train ride. Not long before that, wagon trains crossed through hostile Indian territory as part of the Gold Rush of 1849. US1 is slow and congested, but I am grateful.

Clean Running Water

Turn on the tap and enjoy a drink of fresh water. Only about five percent of the American population had running water at the close of the Civil War in 1878. By the late nineteenth century that figure had increased to 24 percent. The entire urban American population didn't have access to running water until the 1930s. In rural areas, access to running water came about fifteen years later. I am grateful.

Flush Toilets

Had you been born not too long ago, you might be using an outhouse or living in a smelly urban environment that harbored dangerous bacteria and diseases. Flush toilets were introduced in the 1890s. A lot of infrastructure had to get built before sewer lines and waste treatment plants were commonplace. Before that, waste disposal was unsanitary and inconvenient. Gotta go? There's a bathroom down the hall. I am grateful.

Home Computers

Do you complain that your computer is too slow? Home computers didn't become common until the 1980s. I bought my first Macintosh Plus in 1987. It had 1MB of RAM, no hard drive, a 640x480-pixel black and white screen – and it was the most powerful personal computer available. I paid $1799 for it – about what I paid for my 27-inch iMac in 2016. I am grateful.

Traffic Signals

We all curse traffic and traffic signals that are oblivious to the fact that while you're waiting at a red light, nobody's driving the crosswise direction. But imagine what traffic would be like without automated lights and signals. These are relatively recent inventions. The world's first manually operated gas-lit traffic signal was installed in London in December, 1868. It exploded less than a month later, killing its operator. The first automated traffic control system was patented in 1910. It used the words "STOP" and "PROCEED," though neither word lit up. The three-colored traffic signal first appeared in Detroit in 1920. On February 5, 1952, the first "Don't Walk" automatic signs were installed in New York City. Red light cameras are evil, but I am grateful for traffic lights and signs.

Television

How much of your life is rendered in pixels? How many channels do you have? How many hours do you spend staring at a screen?

After World War II, black-and-white TV broadcasting became popular in the United States and Britain; television sets became commonplace in homes, businesses, and institutions. During the 1950s, television was the primary medium for influencing public opinion. Color TV was invented during the 1950s, but flat screens didn't become popular until the 2010s.

I'm a film buff, and I especially love animation. I am grateful.

The Microchip

How many of your toys, gadgets, and tools depend on microchips? The transistor was invented in 1947. In April 1960, Texas Instruments announced multivibrator #502 as the world's first integrated circuit available on the market. It was offered at US$450 per unit or at US$300 for quantities larger than 100 units. However, sales began in the summer of 1961, and the price was higher than announced. Before that, electronics were heavy, expensive, and full of vacuum tubes. I love my digital toys and tools. I am grateful.

Air-Conditioning

How comfortable are you during the summer months? Not long ago, electric fans and open windows might have been your only relief from the relentless heat of September in Miami. During the post-World War II economic boom, residential air conditioning became popular. More than one million units were sold in 1953 alone. During the 1970s, central air was introduced. I am grateful.

The Microwave Oven

Need lunch heated fast? The microwave is a historical newcomer. A large 220-volt wall unit was marketed as a home microwave oven in 1955 for a price of US$1,295 ($12,000 in 2016 dollars), but it did not sell well. In 1967, Amana introduced the first popular home model, the countertop Radarange, at a price of US$495 ($4,000 in 2016 dollars). By 1986, 25 percent of households owned a microwave. I don't use mine much, but when I do, I am grateful.

Refrigeration

Open the fridge and grab a cold one. Help yourself; there's plenty of ice. Most people born before you didn't have this convenience. The first commercial ice-making machine was invented in 1854. In 1913, refrigerators for home use were invented. In 1923 Frigidaire introduced the first self-contained unit. The introduction of Freon in the 1920s expanded the refrigerator market during the 1930s. A 1926 Kelvinator cost anywhere between $350 and $600 – that's $4,721-$8,093 in today's money. Widespread implementation of the familiar-looking refrigerator did not take place until the 1940s, particularly after the end of World War II. Though I lived without refrigeration during my sailing days, that experience makes me all the more thankful whenever I need something kept cool.

The Digital Camera

Point, shoot, and take a picture. There are over four-billion digital cameras in the world. You may be on-camera as you read this. In 1986, Nikon introduced the first digital single-lens reflex (DSLR) camera. In the mid-to-late 1990s, DSLR cameras became common. By the mid-2000s, DSLR cameras had largely replaced film cameras. My digital photo collection includes tens of thousands of images that didn't require film to be developed and paid for. I am grateful.

Textiles and the Availability of Clothing and Fashion

If you live in the US, you've probably never sewn your own clothes, but why bother? You have access to an endless variety of fashions and styles. French tailor, Barthelemy Thimonnier, patented the first workable sewing machine in 1830. Along with the simplification of fashion styles and the increase in the number of women who worked outside the home, by 1910, the industry of ready-made clothing was established in America. Before that, sewing was an important life skill. And before machine-woven cloth became available during the 1800s, animal skins were our best option. I am grateful.

The Wilderness

I have climbed mountains, sailed a wooden boat across the Atlantic, and swum with humpback whales. The environment needs our attention, but this world is still full of amazing and inspiring natural settings. I am grateful.

Recording Technology

Thomas Edison worked with recording sound on wax cylinders back in the 1870s, but consider what recording technology grew into during the past few decades. Not only has sound quality improved remarkably, the sheer volume of music recorded since the 1930s – much of it by people who are now dead – has left our generation with a library of recorded musical history to enjoy and learn from. You will never get to hear Beethoven perform any of his own compositions, but you can hear Sergei Rachmaninoff, and your children will be able to hear The Rolling Stones (assuming Keith Richards doesn't live forever). Even better, we can stream this immense library to our phones and computers. I am grateful.

You Are *So* Lucky

If we round the span of human history to 20,000 years and assume you'll live a hundred years, your life occupies only one-half of one percent of that time. Regardless of how lucky you were to have landed on Earth at this particular time, what are the odds that you are here at all?

Colors

February, 1991

And then, the unspeakable purity and freshness of the air! There was just enough heat to enhance the value of the breeze, and just enough wind to keep the whole sea in motion, to make the waves come bounding to the shore, foaming and sparkling, as if wild with glee.

– Anne Bronte, *Agnes Grey*

VERDANT MAN-O-WAR CAY shines boldly against a turquoise sea on a blue-white winter afternoon. Gumelemi, seagrape, and poisonwood hammocks embrace white colonial houses. High hills encircle the anchorage, protecting the harbour from the sea. On the sea bottom, the dark figure of a nurse shark at rest contrasts with the lighter hues of sand and seagrass. Where everything is remarkable, nothing is remarkable. These colors are the stuff of daily experience.

At anchor in Man-O-War's southeastern harbour, I regret my promise to care for John Nation's cat for two weeks while he visits his mother in Oklahoma. The paralyzing favor has just passed its fifth week when Drew sails into the anchorage on *Walden.*Recognizing *Blue Monk* (by coincidence, she belonged to him many years before), he rows over in his fiberglass Whitehall dinghy, a traditional New England rowing craft – a long glass slipper of a pulling boat with a graceful, swooping shear and a wineglass transom.

When I first met Drew at Dinner Key, he sailed a wooden, double-ended sloop named *Corentina.* Her planks ran stem-to-stern without butt blocks or scarf joints. Drew cruised her up and down the American Atlantic coast and the Caribbean by himself. A capable navigator and a talented carpenter, he made a modest living with a captain's license and a coping saw. Calling upon a wealth of sailing experience, his confident voice rumbled beneath his mustache over his brown beard, relating engaging stories of his many travels and adventures, punctuated by hearty laughter. I often joined him for morning coffee or an occasional moonlight sail. Sometimes, he'd disappear for months at a time but, like so many others, Drew always found himself called back to Dinner Key.

Beaufort, North Carolina was Drew's second home port. On a whim, he would journey into the Gulf Stream alone for the week-long passage as casually as most people head to the store for a carton of milk. He sold *Corentina* when he found a bargain on *Walden,* a fiberglass, cutter-rigged Westsail 32. He quickly hammered her into cruising shape and resumed his wanderings.

Like myself, Drew is an aficionado of the spruce oar as a mode of locomotive power. Most cruisers depend on outboard engines and inflatable dinghies for transport. But while such craft make for fast, convenient transportation, oars always start on a cold morning and require no petrochemical fuel. As with sailing, a seakindly pulling boat, responding to subtle changes in angle and pressure on the oars, inspires a unique joy.

Rowing is a cultivated taste, a skill that comes with practice. Most people can't even stand up in a proper rowing dinghy, but a good oarsman can balance on the breasthook while he steps from his dinghy to the dock, or flip himself from the sea into his boat without shipping water. Internal combustion has its merits but a long rowing craft, like its canvas-bearing counterpart, compels one to slow down, to focus on the journey rather than the destination. Brute force has little to do with proper rowing. With polished technique, one can row at a swift and earnest pace for miles. As the musician's practiced touch squeezes the subtle, sweet essence from a string, an accomplished rower handles his sweeps and his vessel with an intuitive mastery that spirits him effortlessly across the waves.

Drew looks at *Light Blue,* my Chamberlain dory-skiff tethered behind *Blue Monk.* My tender is the same size as his Whitehall. He smiles mischievously. "Would you like to take a row?"

A northeaster is blowing. Even behind the sixty-feet-high coral hills that surround Man-O-War anchorage, brisk gusts of wind kick up a small chop.

"Sure. Where to? I imagine the seas are pretty choppy outside."

"Let's go to a beach, first," Drew suggests, "to clean the dinghies. I hate rowing with a dirty bottom and I still have a few Dinner Key barnacles to get rid of. Then we'll go rowing and end up where we end up." He pauses and grins before continuing. "We don't have to choose a destination to go rowing, do we?"

The question is rhetorical, but the suggestion to clean the dinghies is a good one. I do have some weedy spots on the underside of *Light Blue* though barnacles don't grow in these clear, clean waters.

We row northwest toward town, up the narrow lagoon, past moored sailboats and the docks of white-planked Bahamian houses trimmed with pastel shutters, past paths lined with conch shells and coconut palms, to a small beach where we drag our boats ashore and turn them over. A few minutes with a sharp putty knife and a coarse scrubbing pad consign scrapings of unwanted marine growth to the sand. We flip the dinghies back over, push them into the water, and climb aboard.

Clean, *Light Blue* feels faster, as if freshly oiled. She rows easily, gliding with enthusiasm.

Drew pulls ahead, not quite challenging me to a race, but wordlessly suggesting we put our backs into the pace.

A rocky cut in the side of hairpin-shaped Man-O-War Cay provides a narrow gate for its well-protected anchorage. We exit into the Sea of Abaco.

"There's a coral head in the channel!" Drew remarks, looking down into water that's still fairly clear in spite of being stirred up by the chop.

"The locals know where the rocks are," I explain. "The channel is deep enough so most of them can go over it. The rest know to go around it. I doubt anyone will be coming by to install a marker, dynamite it, or file a complaint."

Drew smiles. He knows how it is in these islands. If you don't know where you're going and you don't keep your eyes open, you don't belong here.

The lee side of Man-O-War is scrub-covered coral – sharp gray rock covered by succulent plants with an overhanging shelf undercut by thousands of years of wave action. The waves are bigger here than in the harbour; they slosh musically under the rocky shelf.

We continue, pulling steadily, breathing hard but working toward a second wind.

Drew looks over to see how I'm doing. *Light Blue* can handle herself in a sea. I row enough and swim enough to stay in good shape.

I'm doing *great.*

We continue around the point to head northeast into the wind, toward the reef and the mighty Atlantic Ocean.

The waves grow bigger. The north wind has put the distant reef in a rage. The wind is lighter than expected, probably gusting to twenty knots, but these waves were sent by far stronger winds from higher latitudes. Driving into wind and sea, we pull up and over the crests. Atlantic swells roll in from the deep, trip over the drop-off, and shatter against the coral ahead of us. A mile off the coast of Man-O-War, the reef line is a seething highway of white foam and exploding silver spray. Immense glass cannonballs detonate against a wall of impenetrable rock.

We pull harder, approaching the coral wall that demarcates the deep Atlantic from the shallow Bahama Banks — the third largest barrier reef on Earth. I wonder if we might not be engaged in a foolhardy contest, but our boats are dry, handling the waves as good pulling craft were designed to. We continue out over turbulent water, our bows facing a sky that fades from pastel blue to hazy white at the horizon.

The cut receives us – a sixty-foot deep, sixty-foot wide hole in the coral battlement worn by time, tide, and geological happenstance. To either side, rocky fingers of dull orange, brown, and green clutch at the sky through the foamy remains of spent waves. Black hills of moving water thunder spectacularly against unyielding coral, hissing and sizzling as they dissipate into rainbow mist. The power surrounding us is awe-inspiring. Many ships have met their ends on this coral; some of them lie in fragmented repose beneath us. How many people have witnessed nature's fireworks at this proximity and lived?

I look for Drew. He's two boatlengths away, on top of a wave, six feet above me.

Blue-black swells crowd through the cut, growing taller and closer together.

Drew drops below me as I'm carried up on the crest of the next wave.

Inside the cut, the swells find no coral to break against. They pile up on themselves as they roll from the deep ocean into the shallow waters.

Where are we? The reef is difficult to make out through the big rollers.

Drew hooks his head to one side, suggesting we turn back. It would not be wise to row past the reef line and miss the cut coming back in; we'd never make it over the coral. We've seen what we came to see. Past this point lies nothing but miles and miles and more miles of cobalt swell.

Atop the next crest, I take a mental bearing on the houses and the white beach of Man-O-War Cay stretching off to the northwest. Hopetown Light guards the coast of Elbow Cay to the east where the Abaco out-island chain curves abruptly south. The next instant, I'm lowered into a valley surrounded by blue, foam-streaked mountains. I time my turn carefully so as not to get caught broadside by the big seas. Long, light oars give us leverage to work with our boats and the tremendous forces surging beneath them. I have an advantage with my higher freeboard. Drew ships an inch of water over his low shear, but manages his turnabout.

We head back.

The seas move faster than our boats, but pulling hard, we can almost match their speed.

Drew synchronizes his pace with a wave.

I follow.

We're surfing!

The pounding reef falls behind.

On this side of the coral, the shallow water pulses with an impressionistic watercolor glow. We glide over sand patches, seagrass beds, and coral gardens, pulling hard, straining to keep pace with the racing seas we ride. The incoming tide runs with the wind, flooding onto the banks, carrying us back to shore.

The swells diminish as we distance ourselves from the coral, but these blue horses are charged with the power of a North Atlantic gale. Large enough to carry us briskly, they are strong enough to capsize our boats if they can catch us abeam. We time each wave, surfing with extended oars to control direction and balance.

Drew stays one wave ahead.

I can't catch him.

We laugh and shout as we charge through the flying rollers.

Exhilarating!

I feel each incoming wave, gauging how the swell will lift me, then pull and turn my tiny boat. By design, we row facing away from our destination. Atop the crests, I glance over my shoulder to take fresh bearings on Man-O-War's rocky southeastern shore. That coast is no place I'd care to land in these conditions, but our course around the island's point is true. After a long few minutes, we round the island to turn into Man-O-War's lee, into the gentle chop behind its rocky shore, over the coral head that sits in the middle of the entrance channel, and past the piling marking the edge of the shoal inside the lagoon.

Seen from the Queen's Highway – the jungle-shaded footpath that runs along the spine of the island – or perhaps from the white porch of a pink-shuttered Bahamian house on the harbour's edge, two sun-darkened figures rowing into Man-O-War Harbour are hardly remarkable, even with a norther blowing and the reef in a rage. Where everything is remarkable, nothing is remarkable. These colors are the stuff of daily experience.

– *The Blue Monk,* 2016

Swimming with Whales

April, 2013

My wife and I and our seven-year-old daughter, Eva, join Conscious Breath Adventures on one of their expeditions to swim with humpback whales on the Silver Bank, ninety miles north of the Dominican Republic. After a flight from Miami, we find ourselves aboard the 138-foot *Sun Dancer II,* pushing north into choppy seas. "It's windier than usual," explains Gene Flipse, our captain. "Weather is always a gamble, but I expect things will calm down; they usually do."

Early the next morning, we are awakened by changes in the sound of the engines as the crew moors our boat behind a protecting band of coral. My family and the others who make up this expedition's complement of sixteen passengers are grateful for the relative quiet and calm. It's still windy – too windy and rough to venture out in pursuit of whales – but this anchorage is much calmer than the open water we crossed to get here. We use the first day to get acquainted, catch up on lost sleep, and learn a bit about humpbacks.

Gene tells us about the whales' annual migration from the deep waters off New England to these *relatively* shallow 100-foot-deep banks where the whales court, mate, and give birth to their calves. We are told to expect to see a range of social behaviors like "pec-slapping" and "breaching."

The next morning, we convene for breakfast. I'm impressed. I'm one of those difficult-to-feed people who are allergic to milk, and when it comes to animal protein, I eat only seafood. The ship's galley accommodates me without complaint. I am well fed and ready to have my first whale experience. It's still blowing briskly, though; I expect we'll have another day of reading and milling about.

But we didn't come here for that. "Suit up!" calls Captain Gene. "Put on your wetsuits, get your gear, and meet on the lower deck in thirty minutes." We make ourselves ready, pulling stretchy neoprene over hands and feet, and adjusting straps on fins and masks. As each of the tenders pulls alongside the mother ship, we transfer over in two groups, find our seats, and head out.

"Call out if you see a whale blow," says Gene. "Humpbacks come to the surface to breathe every twenty minutes or so; the calves breathe every six or seven minutes. When they do, you'll see a misty plume rise from the top of their head. What we're looking for is a mom with a calf. We'll follow for a while and then, if we're fortunate, mom will settle on the bottom and we'll slip into the water to visit with them."

It isn't long before one of our passengers cries, "Ten o'clock; off to the left!"

"I saw it," says Gene. He directs our course around a large coral head that breaks the surface in front of us and pushes the throttles forward. We slow down as we approach the area where we last saw the whale breathe. Gene gives the wheel to his wingman and puts a finger to his lips. "I'll go in first. If there's an opportunity to swim with this whale, I'll motion for you to join me in the water. Slip in *quietly* without a lot of splashing, stay together, and swim slowly toward me on the surface – no diving down, please."

I'm grateful for the "no diving" part. I've been a SCUBA diver for over thirty years, but my wife and daughter are less comfortable, especially as the water is choppy today and a bit murky. Conscious Breath Adventures' expeditions are strictly mask-and-snorkel – and this means that kids and grandparents are able to experience what Gene is about to share with us.

"We've got a mom and calf here," calls Gene. He motions for us to slip into the water. It's *scary* – at least at first. Unless you're Gene who swims in hundred-foot-deep water every day, jumping into deep, murky, choppy waves probably feels a bit like your first skydive. I jump in, adjust my mask, and extend my hand to Eva and Suzanne. Soon, we're all breathing (quickly) through our snorkels, waiting for our bodies to warm the cool seawater that's saturated our wetsuits, and paddling toward Gene.

"Over near you, Dave." I hear Gene call.

I look down and there it is – a *massive* tail. It must be ten or twelve feet wide and only a few feet below me.

I brace myself for a rush of water and take a breath.

The whale jets off with a kick of her tail but I feel nothing. I thought I'd end up spinning in her wake.

The encounter lasts only a moment, but a thought hits me: *She knew I was there!* She was *careful* not to hit me with her tail or blow me back with a powerful current of water.

And thus went my first encounter with a whale – not only in the "forty-foot behemoth" sense of the word, but in the sentient, spiritual sense. The world "careful" implies intention – *care* – and when you find yourself in the presence of a creature that could crush you with a single tail stroke and *consciously* chooses not to, you can't help but feel you have met something big and powerful and *benevolent.*

"I guess this pair didn't want to hang around," says Gene with a shrug. He takes people out here to deliver "the whale experience," but it's early in our week-long expedition and he's optimistic.

Over the coming days, we are not disappointed.

We are treated to a mom and calf who breach continuously for over a half-hour, hurling their bodies almost clear of the water and twisting to look at us in our tiny, fragile boat before they crash down into the sea again. This is National Geographic stuff – Animal Planet – happening a hundred feet off our bow.

A "rowdy group" approaches – a collection of males chasing a female who has already paired with a male "escort." They bump together aggressively, sometimes landing on top of one another. One has a broken dorsal fin; another has a bloody rostrum (the whale's version of a chin). We watch a dozen or more whales charge along just beneath the surface until we find ourselves directly in their path. Though our tiny boat is but a matchstick to the amorous whales, they dive beneath us and continue on. The white patches on their pectoral fins glow brilliant turquoise as they pass sixty-or-more feet beneath us. Even while distracted by their courting instincts, these animals *care* enough to avoid doing us harm. They know we're here.

We snorkel on the reefs, and dive on the wreck of the *Polyxeni,* a freighter that collided with the reef years before and was left there to slowly disintegrate.

We dine in style, catered to by the same crew who accompany us on our daily whale expeditions. Somehow, they summon the strength to dress up after the day's expedition and provide excellent table service.

As we enjoy breakfast and dinner, the big ports on either side of the dining cabin reveal whales passing next to our ship.

"Watch for the green flash at sunset," encourages Captain Gene. We don't see one, but many of his guests have and he has photos to prove that the phenomenon is more than just a nautical legend.

At night we watch the endless stars of the Milky Way from the upper deck.

By our last day on the Silver Banks we've grown accustomed to the boats and the water and the whales. We've taken hundreds of pictures and, bound together by our unique, shared experience, become friends. The water has calmed and cleared. As the daylight fades, our farewell encounter with a mother whale and her calf proves to be the grand finale. Mother whale rests on the bottom, rising occasionally to breathe less than fifty feet from where our group is swimming – close enough to look her in the eye and see that she is looking back. Her calf surfaces repeatedly, almost within touching distance, and then returns to the bottom to tuck in close to her mother.

After forty-five minutes of this remarkable encounter, I swim back to the tender and climb aboard. Suzanne and Eva have grown comfortable and confident in the water with the whales and the snorkeling gear. Eva boldly approaches the baby whale; Suzanne grabs Eva's flipper to pull her back. I am as pleased to watch my wife's and daughter's newfound confidence as I was to swim with the humpbacks.

Looking a seventy-thousand-pound whale in the eye is profound and powerful. Perhaps we all have whales in our lives, and we are all afraid to get in the water with them. Few are blessed with the opportunity to stare into the eye of a live, non-metaphorical whale, but having taken that swim, made that connection, and watched my family and fellow passengers, I know we are all better for our experience.

High school sketch, circa 1980

Souls and Stories

1987

INANIMATE OBJECTS capable of sustaining a soul merit elevation in status from "it" to "he" or "she," and are often given proper names. Musical instruments, vehicles, and boats, especially wooden boats fabricated from living things, are traditionally named. Gear that works well long after its expected lifetime may earn a familiar title. Any machine betraying the presence of an interior ghost may thus join the ranks of the animata.

Now that I own a sailboat moored in the Dinner Key Anchorage, I need a way to get out to her. My boss's girlfriend is willing to part with an eight-foot fiberglass dinghy with a two-piece mast, a pair of oars, and a good sail for $100. Small black vinyl letters on her transom declare her name, *Artemisia Gentileschi* – after the 17th century painter. I lash the boat to the roof of *Little Red Riding Hood,* my 1969 Dodge Dart – white with a red hood. The oars barely fit, lying diagonally from the passenger side dashboard to the deck behind the back seat. The front seat will still accommodate a passenger as long as she doesn't mind a pair of oars crossing her left shoulder.

At the dinghy dock, I lift *Artemisia Gentileschi* from the roof of *Little Red Riding Hood* and drop her in the bay so I can row myself to *Blue Monk*. Maybe this is Dinner Key's secret source of color. My modes of transportation sound like a children's story about baroque art on acid jazz.

The weekend is over. My new, old boat is clean. The mildew has been scrubbed away. The rotten teak grab rails are gone; I bought replacements from Shell Lumber and put the first few coats of varnish on them. After five more coats, I'll bolt them to the cabin top on either side of the teak main hatch I've likewise begun to restore.

I still can't believe I have my own sailboat, my own private apartment in the secret floating village, my own key to a hidden doorway leading to an alternate dimension. I row back through the anchored boats toward the channel to the dinghy dock. My guitar lies in its case on the back seat.

While rowing past the channel marker at the edge of the world as you know it, I narrowly miss colliding with another dinghy. Black, wooden and tubby with firehose rub rails, the craft is piloted by a tall, lanky, fortyish man with short sandy hair and a friendly smile. Propped up in his stern is an instrument case.

"Hey banjo man, can you play that thing?"

"Yes, sir," he responds. "Can you play a good rhythm guitar?"

"I like to think so. I'm Dave. I just put my boat out in the middle anchorage."

"We're neighbors, then. I'm John – John Nation. Come on out and visit me on *Zebra Dun*. She's the only boat in the anchorage with no spreaders on her masts. Know what a schooner is?"

"Not exactly."

I'm embarrassed; I should know these things. I silently guess spreaders are the crosspieces seen on most sailboat masts. I know the difference between a sloop and a ketch, but I wasn't in class the day they covered schooners, cutters, and yawls. John perceives the inexperience on my twenty-three-year-old face and enlightens me. "A schooner and a ketch both have two or more masts. A ketch has the taller mast in front. On a schooner, the taller mast is in back. The *Zebra Dun* is white with black bulwarks and tanbark sails; you can't miss her. When are you coming out again?"

"Next weekend; I have to go back to school tomorrow."

"School? Nuts. Whatcha studying?"

"Jazz guitar."

"Well, I guess you *can* play that thing. Tell you what – I have a hand-cranked cedar bucket ice-cream maker on board. Round up a bag of rock salt and we'll put us a party together next Sunday."

Dinner Key has a way of assimilating you into its great patchwork quilt. Yesterday, I stood on the periphery – a jazz guitar student working at a software company – looking in on a strange collection of eccentric storybook characters. Today, I lead a secret life on weekends with homemade ice cream parties on Biscayne Bay. Whatever draws people to Dinner Key is powerful enough to break the gravitational pull of traditional, terrestrial life. Therein lies a story – *your* story. I can't say mine amounts to much yet, but having found its way into a marvelous anthology, I sense it will only get better.

John smiles, nods his head warmly, then slips around the channel marker to disappear into the anchorage.

The week goes by slowly.

I'm no longer me.

I'm a tiny alien sitting in somebody's head, peering out through somebody's eyes, saying the things he's supposed to say. The classrooms and the office and the apartment are not of my home planet.

During the week, I do some research. "Bulwarks" are tall wooden rails that extend the height of a ship's sides above the deck line.

"Tanbark" sails are reddish brown.[22]

Sunday afternoon, I tie a float to *Blue Monk's* mooring line and cast off, motoring over to the white schooner with the tall black bulwarks and the raked-back main mast. I tie fenders[23] alongside my hull and raft up to John's forty-foot pirate ship. Built in a Texas back yard of mahogany planks, she's a replica of a 1911 Nova Scotia Tancook Whaler fishing schooner. If my little fiberglass sloop is the moon, this is Saturn – a good distance farther away from the straight-and-level, clock-punching, rent-paying world I find myself estranged from.

John gives me a tour of his ship. A long tiller extends from her rudder to a standing well in the stern that serves as a cockpit. Forward of that is a low aft cabin with a roof raised a few short inches above the deck. Down below, John's sleeping quarters are only high enough to sit up in. On the port side, a double bunk complements shelves and lockers to starboard. Steps descend between them. Light scatters from glass deck prisms overhead. Growing up, I spent much of my free time in a treehouse I cobbled together in my back yard; this is the nautical equivalent.

The main mast comes up through the deck just forward of the aft cabin. A bridge deck of mahogany boards introduces the raised, main cabin trunk. John slides the hatch forward. We descend into a charming wooden saloon[24] tall enough to stand up in only if I hunch over. Bronze ports[25] and brass lanterns add a traditional touch. Varnished mahogany beams accentuate the neat, white planks of the overhead. A varnished shear plank glows where her white cabin sides meet the deck. *Zebra Dun's* small but comfortable interior reflects her builder's skill as a shipwright and his respect for nautical tradition.

The *Zebra Dun's* kitchen is in her bow, between the main cabin and the chain locker all the way forward. Though cooking is an endeavor traditionally practiced standing up, John Nation's sensible design for his ship's galley places the stove, oven, countertop and pantry within arms' reach, enabling the chef to sit comfortably while preparing a meal.

I take in the *Zebra Dun's* interior with my hands on my knees, feeling like Gulliver in Lilliput. "Sit down and get comfortable," John urges.

"You could have built the cabin trunk six inches higher, no? I'm sure you..."

"Of course I thought of it; I'm six-foot-two – and I was married back when I built the boat. My wife *definitely* thought of it, but next time you're coming or going, visualize a tall cabin while you're looking at the lines of the boat. Tancook Whalers were originally designed as open fishing boats. You can get away with a small cabin trunk, but if you build the houses too tall, the boat will look like she's got two refrigerators lying on deck. Headroom is like love; it's nice to have, but a lot of crimes have been committed in its name."

Aside from being an able boat carpenter, John is an ex-planetarium director, a talented writer, a former administrator for the Oklahoma City Ballet, and an authority on classical music. His quick mind stores endless obscure facts and details. On his galley countertop is a small toy. "My titanothere," John explains. "A plastic, prehistoric rhinoceros I found on the street in Coconut Grove. *Brontotheriidae* are more closely related to horses than rhinos, if you care to get technical about the taxonomy, but I figured I'd give it a home on the *Zebra Dun;* everything else is a relic or a reissue. If you haven't figured it out yet, I was born a century or two later than I should have been."

A small Siamese cat crawls onto John's lap and purrs under his chin. "This is Kipling," he explains, "ship's cat."

"And the name of the boat?"

"*Zebra Dun* was the name of a wild bucking horse in an old cowboy poem. As the story goes, the cowboys are sitting around the fire when a stranger comes along who speaks just a little too fancy and educated for their liking. He needs a horse, so they play a trick on him and give him the Zebra Dun."

My host closes his eyes and recites:

We could see the tops of mountains under Dunny's every jump,
But the stranger he was growed there just like the camel's hump.
The stranger sat upon him and twirled his black mustache
Just like a summer boarder waiting for his hash.
He thumped him in the shoulders and spurred him when he whirled

And hollered to them punchers, "I'm the wolf of the world!"
When the stranger had dismounted and was once more upon the ground,
We knew he was a thoroughbred and not a dude from town.

"I grew up on a farm in Oklahoma, but my mother was a poet and I've always been fascinated by just about everything. I'm an astronomer and a writer but I'm still a cowboy at heart. I figure the name connects me to the boat."

We hear a commotion outside and go topside to investigate.

"John Nation!" calls a cheerful voice from an approaching sailboat. "Prepare to be boarded."

"I'll be hot-dipped!" exclaims John. "It's Bob Treat."

We fasten dock lines to deck cleats. Soon, three vessels are rafted together on the bay a half-mile from shore.

Social awkwardness is absent out here; you can safely assume everyone is an eccentric worth talking to. Meeting new people in Dinner Key Anchorage is like going to a potluck book exchange. A great deal usually gets said before the conversation ever meanders around to "What do you do in *real life?*" The sarcasm inherent in the question is lost on no one. Bob works as a pilot for dubiously named Midway Airlines. He sails and plays guitar when he's not flying. In his forties, he's jocular, thin-haired, and stocky with a boyish and sharply intelligent gleam in his eye. Today, he successfully absconded with a group of bluegrass musicians after their performance at a local festival. Afloat at Dinner Key, they're lost in an alternate universe.

They hand instrument cases carefully over the rope rails. I stack them on top of John's aft cabin before assisting their owners aboard. Pam's here with her banjo. Two girls play fiddles. There's a mandolin. Bob plays guitar. I have mine and, of course, John's got his banjo. Before long, we're arranged on deck on chairs improvised from sail bags, singing, playing and taking turns cranking the ice-cream maker.

The ice cream is delicious, the music transporting.

We swap songs, jokes, and stories as a red sun sets the clouds on fire.

"I'm reminded," says John, in between *Hot Corn Cold Corn* and *The Wabash Cannonball,* "of a time years ago when the Oklahoma City Ballet did a *Nutcracker* tour at Christmas. I was driving the bus and it broke down. We pulled over by a little park in a small town at two in the morning to try to find the problem and get back on the road. With the engine out, things got pretty cold pretty fast. Before long, we had twenty costumed dancers stomping their feet and rubbing their hands trying to keep warm. With nothing else to do, they put on a complete performance of *The Nutcracker* right there in the park. Not a soul was around to see, hear, or know about it. Anyone walking in the park the next morning had no idea that something spontaneous, extraordinary and beautiful had happened there during the night."

Three hours later, after returning *Blue Monk* to her anchors, I row *Artemisia Gentileschi* past the red channel marker at the edge of the world as you know it to the dinghy dock. I slide my oars through the passenger door of *Little Red Riding Hood* and return to my apartment that has no name.

– *The Blue Monk,* 2016

Roaring Forties Jim

December, 1990

A story I shall now relate
About my buddy Jim
Who, while most preferred to walk
Was more inclined to swim

Though friends and duty pulled at him
'twas pretty plain to me
That my friend Jim could not resist
The calling of the sea

Now Jim, at home, was loved by all
A respected and prosperous man
A nice Jewish boy who went crazy they say
And set off in a small trimaran

Death of the Guitar

"He'll weary of it soon," they said
"That boat is awfully small"
But in spite of all their prophesy
Jim was having himself a ball

It's true his vessel wasn't large
And tiny to some she seemed
But she made up in speed what she lacked in size
And o'er the seas she screamed

Roaring Forties was the name
With which Jim christened his craft
And any vessels she approached
Were soon left far abaft

I first espied the *Roaring Forties*
Anchored at Green Turtle Cay
And thought her to be as strange a craft
As ever sailed the sea

I sung out loud and hailed to her
"Ahoy *Roaring Forties,*" I roared
And through the companionway came Jim
And Wild Irish Bill was aboard

And that's how I first saw the trimaran
And how upon a whim
I came into the company
Of *Roaring Forties* Jim

Jim told me of his travels and of
How when the wind did blow
He'd sailed for high adventure
In the isles of Abaco

But soon the old north wind piped up
And threatened to blow a gale
The seas grew rough and sealed off
The passage they call "the whale"

And since that treacherous passage lay
Right dead upon our course
We stayed safe in the lee of Green Turtle Cay
And talked till we were hoarse

I asked of him, my buddy Jim
How long 'fore he planned to go?
He looked around and then replied
"Perhaps a month or so"

"I see," I said, trying to appear nonchalant
(Though I chuckled inwardly)
For a month is hardly a moment
To a man upon the sea

The wind died down; we passed through the whale
And Jim and I stayed in touch
But a month soon passed, and did Jim prepare to go?
I think not much

His friends up north came down to see
What the long delay was about
But I'll venture to guess they went home as confused
As when they'd first set out

But Jim, he sailed onward
For even a grown man must
Yield one day to the callings
Of his boyhood wanderlust

So, if you are kin to Jim
Or friend or officemate
Don't let his absence make you feel
Abandoned or irate

Open up your heart instead
And try to feel glad
That in times of TV and microwaves
Adventures are still being had

Death of the Guitar

Be tolerant and patient
And be relieved to know
That Jim will only be here
For another month or so

A Trip to Elliot Key

August 21, 1992

Bud Maddock has a silver streak in his reddish beard, perhaps to compensate for the silver he lacks in his blue denim pockets. He made some money years ago as a Haliburton engineer developing new oil drilling technologies but when the company downsized him out the door, he put most of his savings into *Antigone*, a forty-six-foot ketch. Anything left over went into getting her ready to go to sea. Forsaken after years of loyal service to industry, he returned the gesture and went cruising, landing as drifters are prone to do in the anchorage at Dinner Key to pass his time reading classics and making plans to head farther south after hurricane season.

Saturday. Boats in the anchorage float languidly on still water. A hazy, blue sky joins its own reflection on the flat-calm bay, obscuring the horizon south of Key Biscayne. Vessels farther out in the anchorage appear to hover low in the air above the water. To the west, a dark mushroom cloud climbs over the distant Everglades.

Aboard *Antigone,* the electric fans hum. The windscoop hangs limp in the hot, still August air. Bud makes himself a late breakfast to a recording of Prokofiev piano sonatas and then, standing on the aft deck, he scrapes his skillet overboard while studying the seagrass through the clear water. A Cassiopeia jellyfish throbs upside down on the bottom beneath the spreading rainbow sheen of vegetable oil fallen from the frying pan. Mangrove snapper flash by, grabbing scraps of dry egg, sloshing noisily as they attack pieces floating on the surface.

Bud places the skillet in a white five-gallon bucket to soak and chases it with a stream of dish soap from a yellow plastic squeeze-bottle. Standing in the cockpit under the blue canvas Bimini top, he slowly inhales the thick summer air. A powerboat blasts out the north channel, its engine obscuring all but the crisp hissing of cymbals from its blaring stereo. Its wake creeps across the anchorage and continues south across the bay towards Coral Gables, a long ripple gliding across a hot mirror.

Stepping below, he lies down on the starboard settee, aims a fan at his face, closes his eyes, and loses himself in the delirious mathematical intricacies of Sonata Number 7.

Just past one o'clock, the flapping of the sailcloth windscoop tied over the open forward hatch awakens him.

Wind!

Ascending the companionway ladder to the cockpit, Bud yawns and stretches. Patches of rippled water fill in the bay. Within minutes, the waves build to a light chop, shattering the reflection of the summer sky into sparkling shards of deeper blue, throwing the once obscure sea horizon into sharp relief. A few thunderheads still prowl the shore far to the west but the morning's stifling heat has risen, circulating the air. Afternoon winds bring deliverance from the morning's stifling heat.

Time to get out of here.

Donning sunglasses and a floppy canvas sailor's hat, Bud starts up the diesel, looking over the stern to ensure cooling water is spraying out with the engine exhaust as it should. Satisfied, he strips the mainsail cover, folds it neatly and stows it in the starboard cockpit locker. He tosses his anchor lines overboard and marks them with buoys improvised from inflatable boat fenders, then motors *Antigone* out past the anchored boats. After steering around the floats and lines of a few stone crab traps, he walks forward to the mast to hoist his big main sail. Then, from the cockpit, he releases the line that controls the roller furling gear and winches in the starboard sheet, pulling open the big white jib like a gigantic window shade. *Antigone* grabs the wind, heels, and gathers speed. Passing the buoy marking the shoal at Middle Ground to port, he steers south, letting the engine idle while he hauls up the mizzen sail before finally pulling the fuel shutoff.

Ah…silence.

He pours a glass of red wine and lets his thoughts drift as he watches the compass. The wind is light but easterly, favorable to his southerly course. With her sails balanced, *Antigone* requires little steering. Bud walks forward to stand at the bow, watching the seagrass drift beneath him. The buildings of downtown Miami and the strange, towering gantries that load and unload shipping containers at the port recede in his wake. A dolphin surfaces to breathe next to his boat. She makes eye contact with him before continuing on. Key Biscayne and Stiltsville drift by to port. Soldier Key's details grow sharper on the horizon, then the Ragged Keys appear and then Boca Chita Key with its tiny lighthouse. Away from the City, farther into Biscayne National Park, the water grows clearer and bluer; not quite so clear and blue as in the so-close-yet-so-far-away Bahamas, but still startlingly different, more closely resembling descriptions of Biscayne Bay given by old-timers who recall a body of water unsullied by street water runoff and urban development.

With binoculars, Bud scans the southern horizon for the two pairs of red and green channel markers that indicate the dredged channel across shallow Featherbed Bank. Tidal crosscurrents are strong here; the markers appear to be moving on their own as he steers *Antigone* through the narrow stripe of deep water between the knee-deep shallows. Once through, he adjusts his course to port, higher into the wind toward the shoreline of Elliot Key, hauling in the sheets to accommodate the windward course. *Antigone* heels to starboard. Bud moves to the higher, port side of the cockpit where he can see ahead past the sails.

The wind is still light; the journey has been pleasurable but slow. It's near sundown when Bud rounds up into the wind to anchor over shallow, sandy bottom in the lee of the island, far enough away so the island's infamous mosquitoes won't be a bother. The breeze is cooling. The sun is low – not so penetrating as in the afternoon. The water is clear, blue and inviting. After placing a pot of rice on the stove to boil, he strips off his clothes and jumps into the refreshing water to cool off. Then, wrapping himself in a towel, he pours another glass of Merlot, exchanges the spent Prokofiev tape for Chopin and lies back on a comfortable cockpit cushion to read.

"What fantastic luck," says Bud aloud to himself. "It's an absolutely gorgeous day and I'm the only one here."

The eye of Hurricane Andrew roared over Elliot Key the day after Bud's arrival. He was airlifted off the boat by a Coast Guard helicopter and returned after the storm to find his boat had been carried – probably by a tornado – well into the island's interior. There, due to bureaucratic incompetence on the part of the Biscayne National Park leadership, he spent the next two years living with the raccoons and mosquitoes until a change of park service command empowered him to refloat his vessel.

Home

2009

"So we beat on, boats against the current, borne back ceaselessly into the past."

— F. Scott Fitzgerald, *The Great Gatsby*

MY FRIEND MILLER has been paying dock rent in Hollywood, Florida. His fortunes have changed; such luxuries are no longer affordable. On my suggestion, we motor his small sloop down the Intracoastal Waterway to the free anchorage in Miami. We make hasty preparations to leave after dark on a windless Friday night. The running lights don't work. The VHF radio would if the battery wasn't dead.

Proceeding south down the waterway past tall buildings, luxury homes, marinas, and mangroves, we alert drawbridges to our presence with a horn affixed to a can of compressed air.

3:30 am – A chill penetrates the air. We pass the *Miami Herald* Building, a sleeping downtown, the port of Miami, the open mouth of the Miami River and tall buildings on Brickell Avenue – all bathed in stark, yellow light, exuding an inaudible yet powerful electric hum, the snoring of a gigantic urban rhinoceros masked by the drone of the outboard motor. Off to port, Virginia Key is pitch-dark save for a few lights along the shore of the Miami Marine Stadium – an abandoned edifice perhaps better likened to a white elephant than a sleeping rhinoceros – but this is Miami; such travesties are not uncommon here. Ahead of us rises Rickenbacker Causeway Bridge, an arch of light, gateway to the open waters of Biscayne Bay. A field of electric stars on the shoreline moves slowly behind the flashing channel markers. We strain our eyes to find them.

"I see a red flasher at one o'clock. Aim a few points to starboard."

A moment later, Miller sees the marker, too. We alter course to align ourselves with the channel and the approaching bridge.

Even at this very late, very early hour, tires *swoosh* across the concrete leviathan above us. To either side of us, wooden catwalks girdle massive pylons supporting the span.

We're through.

Darkness.

The moon has long since set.

The sky is overcast.

Biscayne Bay is not only dark, it's foggy – unusual weather. Some indeterminable distance ahead, channel markers throw vapor-refracted halos of red and green. Hazy lights of buildings shimmer to starboard, but mostly, our path leads into a black abyss; we may as well be headed straight down. Miller is not so much nervous as reality-stricken. He trusts me. He knows I've done some sailing. He doesn't know I find it scary, too – *still.* I've just learned to press on. We're navigating a small boat in the middle of a black, windless night, motoring with a diminishing fuel supply into open water away from the familiar gridlines of civilization. *It's okay,* I quietly assure myself. *Not too far to go.* Perhaps I'm selfishly curious to know if I can still find my old home port after all this time.

Dead calm.

I consider dropping anchor in the lee of Rickenbacker Causeway to wait for daylight before completing the final few miles of our journey but I still the impulse. If a barge is moving across this darkness, I'd rather be awake and ready to take evasive action. If we get lost or run aground, morning will arrive soon enough. The fog will lift. The tide will rise. We'll finish our journey.

Logic wins. Fear and doubt retreat.

We continue into the black.

"Off to starboard, over by Vizcaya, there's a shoal we want to avoid." I gesture into the foggy darkness. "Let's continue south for another twenty minutes and then alter course gradually toward shore. Hopefully, as we get closer, we'll pick out some recognizable buildings in Coconut Grove and the masts of the boats at Dinner Key." Miller nods and smiles. He's enjoying the lunacy of this, the sheer incongruity between daily life and this crazy stab into nothing's eye.

We stare across glistening black, fog-shrouded water through the haze of four-in-the-morning eyes into the distant glow ashore. Familiar reference points elude me, hiding in nebulous shapes and clusters of light. "Turn a bit more to starboard," I suggest. "I think we're past the shoal now. Let's get closer; hopefully I can make out something familiar."

We alter course and carry on.

Time harmonizes with the oddly musical hum of the outboard – the unending meditative chant of a mechanical Zen monk, a repeated mantra I can't quite make out. We don't bother to check how much fuel remains. No wind blows to offer an alternative mode of locomotion. If we run out of fuel, we'll anchor and wait. The wind will blow again eventually; it always does.

"This must be Dinner Key Channel. See the marker lights? Our boat has shallow-enough draft to sail across the channel way out here, but the water gets shallow on the south side closer to shore – 'Idiot Shoal,' they call it." We cross the channel and make our turn.

A form appears out of the gloom ahead, a sleeping sailboat. The white hull and darkened ports approach like a ghost in the mist.

Another appears.

We throttle back to slow our progress.

A battered powerboat covered with old dinghies and marine junk squats on the black water, listing precariously beneath the veil of fog. Boats appear around us now – abandoned hulks, a beautiful ketch, a high-tech trimaran hovering like a gigantic water-bug, a menagerie of old and new, rich and poor, promise and betrayal, dreams forgotten, realized and clung to, tragedy, comedy, hope, desperation, trash, treasure, jetsam, flotsam, wood, fiberglass, and canvas.

"Welcome to Dinner Key Anchorage," I say. "The world as you know it ends here."

Someone said that to me here once a very long time ago.

Ethereal boats pass in and out of the gloom as we continue toward shore.

As if tiptoeing stealthily past a ring of sleeping fairies in an ancient forest, we glide between the scattered boats. Miller is awake now. Certainly, slipping from a black abyss into a secret anchorage is surprising and surreal but that's not really *it*. There are people here – unusual people, people who choose to be in this otherworldly place, people who must therefore be *different*. Within a half-mile of the urban sprawl of Miami, hidden behind a few low islands littered with storm-tossed mangroves and gnarled casuarina pines and broken hulls, lies a secret floating village.

Miller can't know yet. He only senses something's different. That's good enough for now. All will make itself apparent. It wasn't me who brought him here. He's another one, caught like the ocean by the gravity of a prankster moon and pulled like the tide to Dinner Key.

We leave the slumbering hulks and hulls behind to pass through an empty field of small, white buoys closer to shore. "This all used to be anchorage," I explain. "Now, it's a mooring field – floating parking meters for 'respectable' boaters. Most of the original anchorage boats have left or moved farther out or off to the sides of the field. They don't want to pay to anchor and the City still hasn't officially opened the moorings. This area's been sitting empty for months."

I know exactly where we are now.

I sense the shadows of the souls of boats and people who sailed on but never left this place.

The channel marker at the entrance to the marina flashes green. We pass into a realm washed in waxy, incandescent light. After turning to starboard between the piers and the islands, we round the point of the northernmost one and head a short way out to a small, shallow cove. We used to call this 'trimaran cove' but only one mastless trimaran anchors here now.

The splash of the anchor and the rattle of running chain signify the end of our journey. Sharp tugs on the line set the flukes securely into the seagrass.

Miller shuts down the engine.

Silence settles over us, enveloping us as surely as the fog.

I am home.

– *The Blue Monk,* 2016

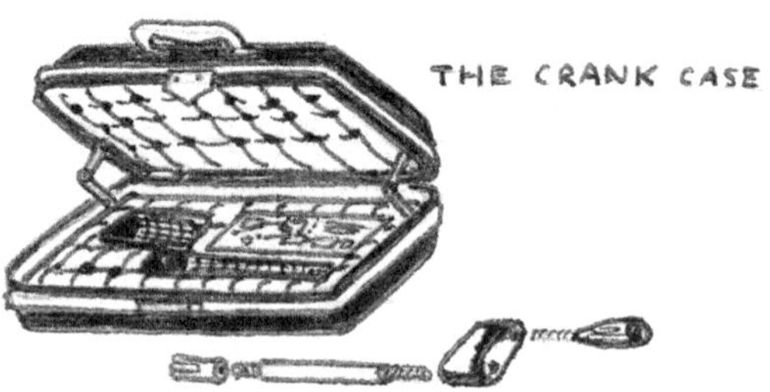

High school sketch, circa 1980

Endnotes

1 http://www.realchristmastrees.org/dnn/Education/Quick-Tree-Facts

2 http://www.religioustolerance.org/xmas_tree.htm

3 http://www.theholidayspot.com/christmas/history/mistletoe.htm

4 http://inhabitat.com/santa-and-the-shrooms-the-real-story-behind-the-design-of-christmas/

5 *Double-ended* – A double-ended vessel has a pointed bow and also a pointed stern.

6 *Lapstraked* planks (a strake is a board) are arranged like shingles where the bottom of one plank overlaps the top of the plank below it.

7 *Hammock* – a hardwood hammock is a tropical forest, not something you sleep in

8 *Conch* – (pronounced konk) are large sea snails with attractive spiral shells. Conch meat is a staple of the Bahamian diet and one of the country's major exports.

9 The *head* is a ship's lavatory or literally, the toilet

10 A *topmast* is a mast extension used on traditional sailing craft.

11 Traditional sailing vessels often have a *bowsprit*, a horizontal spar that extends forward from the bow of the boat. It's supported by *shrouds* on the sides and by a *bobstay* underneath.

12 The *binnacle* is the post upon which the compass and ship's wheel are mounted.

13 A *heptangle* is a rounded rectangle.

14 The DEA is the United States Drug Enforcement Agency

15 This story previously told in *Waves* by Dave Bricker, 2010

16 *On her beam-ends* means heeled over on her side so the deck is almost vertical.

17 *Spars* are masts, booms, gaffs and similar poles used on a sailing vessel

18 My music library included the original and second Glenn Gould recordings of Bach's *Goldberg Variations, Standards Volume I* by Keith Jarrett, Leo Kottke's *Six and Twelve-String Guitars,* a Frank Zappa tape and others. I can still play those tapes in my head, note for note, as clearly and vividly as if they were playing aloud.

19 *Painter* – the line affixed to the bow of a dinghy used to secure it to a boat or dock

20 A *ceiling* on a boat consosts of wooden slats between the hull planks and the cabin's interior

21 A *turning block* is a pulley used to direct sheetlines from a sail to the winches that adjust them.

22 *Tanbark* – In the days of cottons sails, some sailcloth was tanned – dipped in tannins derived from tree bark – to protect them from rot, mold and mildew. The process turned the sails a red-brown color.

23 *Fenders* – Durable, inflatable fenders are hung between two boats or between a boat and the dock to keep them from banging together. Fenders also make convenient buoys for anchor lines.

24 *Saloon* – (pronounced "salon") is a vessel's main cabin.

25 *Ports* – Windows on a boat

About the Author

Inspired by true tales of adventure, Dave Bricker spent fifteen years living afloat. He logged thousands of solo sailing miles and an Atlantic crossing in search of stories.

An award-winning speaker, author, and MFA graphic designer, he helps forward-thinking leaders and teams craft engaging messages across a variety of media. He's also a pretty good a jazz guitarist.

His StorySailing® approach to business storytelling – speaking, writing, design, technology, and publishing – transforms the way audiences and organizations connect with clients, colleagues, and opportunity.

Ask about keynote presentations, workshops, and coaching services, and subscribe to the StorySailing® blog at www.storysailing.com.

Other Books by Dave Bricker

The Dance: a Novel

Waves: a Novel

Currents: a Novel

The One-Hour Guide to Self-Publishing: Straight Talk for Fiction and Nonfiction Writers About Producing and Marketing Your Own Books (out of print)

The Writer's Guide to Powerful Prose

The Blue Monk: A Memoir

The Story Story: A Voyage Through the Islands of Connection and Engagement for Writers, Speakers, Professionals, and Visionaries

The Publisher's Guide to Book Anatomy

StorySailing®: A Guide to Storytelling for Speakers, Trainers, & Coaches

Because independent writers and publishers should be held to the same high standards as the mainstream publishing industry, I encourage you to post an honest and objective review of this book on Amazon.com or the online bookstore of your choice.

Thank you,

—Dave Bricker

www.ingramcontent.com/pod-product-compliance
Lightning Source LLC
Chambersburg PA
CBHW081126300726
48982CB00005B/857